IS PSYCHOLOGY THE MAJOR FOR YOU?

Planning for your undergraduate years

Edited by Paul J. Woods

With Charles S. Wilkinson

AMERICAN PSYCHOLOGICAL ASSOCIATION

Library of Congress Cataloging-in-Publication Data

Woods, Paul J., 1930-
   Is psychology the major for you?

   Bibliography: p.
   1. Psychology—Vocational guidance—United
States. 2. Psychology—Study and teaching—United
States.
I. Wilkinson, Charles, 1956-   . II. Title.
BF76.W66   1987   150′.23′73   87-18740
ISBN 0-912704-78-0

Copies may be ordered from:
Order Department
P.O. Box 2710
Hyattsville, MD 20784

Published by the
American Psychological Association, Inc.
1200 Seventeenth Street, N.W.
Washington, DC 20036

Printed in the United States of America

CONTENTS

Part **3**   **Psychology majors in the workplace: traditional and
             unconventional careers**

Preface

Each year thousands of students graduate from college with a bachelor's degree in psychology, and many students are required to take at least one year of psychology in order to obtain any degree. Why? Because an understanding of psychology provides an individual with a greater capacity for understanding the ways in which human beings interact and a greater appreciation for how one's own behavior affects others. Most students who graduate with a degree in psychology go on to the world of work in business, industry, organizations, and homemaking; some continue their studies and seek an advanced degree before going on.

This volume, which grew out of *The Psychology Major: Training and Employment Strategies* (APA, 1979), is devoted to answering the question "Is psychology the major for you?" from the student's viewpoint. In particular, it is addressed to those who are considering, or have chosen, psychology as a major field of study but who may not plan on becoming professional psychologists (that is, may not go on to pursue a master's- or doctoral-level degree in the field).

Deciding what students need to know about their courses of study and what their advisers need to know is not an easy task. Both share an interest in information on how a degree can be obtained and what can be done with it once a student graduates. However, the student is the person who must decide ultimately on the major course of study that he or she will undertake, and for those who are seeking only a bachelor's degree (or who think that the BA will be the end of their studies), that decision is of particular immediate importance.

Is Psychology the Major for You? is designed to help you, the student, decide whether a degree in psychology will prepare you for the career you wish to pursue or identify what kinds of careers you could pursue once you obtain a degree in psychology. The volume provides information on how to decide on psychology as a major, the value of a psychology BA as a liberal arts degree both for the student's development as an individual and as preparation for a variety of careers, how to make use of career counseling (and make up for its deficiencies), how to find a job, and how to survive as a newly hired employee. Although this volume concentrates on the needs of those pursuing a bachelor of arts degree, selected information on graduate study is also provided. Students with concerns about sex differences, ethnicity, and reentry into study after being away from school for some years will find Part 6 of particular value. Students also will find additional resources (books, journal articles, organizations) compiled in chapter 23.

Much of what is written here also will be valuable to students who wish to pursue degrees in areas other than psychology, because many of the same principles apply for any student who wishes to select, pursue, and fulfill the dream of obtaining a useful degree and a job in which he or she uses to the fullest extent those skills learned in college.

By early 1988, the American Psychological Association will publish a volume specifically prepared for advisers and counselors. This book will provide faculty and placement advisers with additional information that will help them to help students make the all-

important decision about what degrees to pursue.

As you use this volume, you may find that some questions were not answered that could have been, or that areas of greatest concern to you were not addressed. Your comments and reactions are welcome and will help us prepare the adviser's volume.

The study of psychology provides an understanding of one's own behavior and the behavior of others. It also provides an awareness of ways of viewing, analyzing, measuring, and changing human behavior that differ from those learned in the study of other disciplines. This perspective can be intellectually interesting by itself; for students it may also be quite valuable in their work after college. Whether the skills learned are used directly in an area devoted to human services, or to help a person manage other people, to add a different perspective on the problems facing business and industry, or to provide a means of living a better life, a degree in psychology can form a strong foundation upon which to build personal and professional accomplishments. We hope that *Is Psychology the Major for You?* helps you make the correct decision for you, and, if your decision is to pursue a degree in psychology, that it provides you with the guidance you need about the right first steps to take toward a rewarding career.

Paul J. Woods
Hollins College

A word on how this volume was written

In 1984, a group of psychologists, some of whom contributed to the 1979 edition of *The Psychology Major: Training and Employment Strategies*, were asked to participate in a revision of that volume. All shared a common interest in helping students better prepare themselves to pursue a degree in psychology. Once the manuscripts were received and comments were provided by other psychologists and educators, it was recognized by all that what was really needed and, indeed, what was actually in hand, were two separate books—one for students and one for advisers. The decision was made to develop the two books separately, beginning with the student volume, now called *Is Psychology the Major for You?* Manuscripts from among those developed for the revision of *The Psychology Major* were reviewed and relevant content selected for the student volume. This substantive material has been carefully edited and rewritten to meet the needs of students. A second volume, designed for advisers and based on those same initial manuscripts, is now in preparation for publication in early 1988.

Acknowledgment

A special thanks to the production staff at APA, especially to Brenda Bryant, who supervised the project and whose ideas and guidance determined the scope and nature of the book; to Deanna D'Errico and Donna Stewart for their expert editing and restructuring of the book; to freelancers Katherine Hoskins and Juliette Ayisi for their copyediting and proofreading; and to Patricia Harding-Clark and Pam Presar for their clerical input and insightful suggestions.

What are 40,000 psychology majors going to do next year?

In 1987, more than 40,000 students will graduate with bachelor's degrees in psychology (U.S. Department of Education, 1982). What are they going to do? Many will go on to work. Many will go on to graduate school. Some will do both. A much smaller group will do neither. Let's examine the first of these groups in greater detail in order to better answer the question of what happens to psychology majors after they graduate.

The work group

Nearly 50% of all psychology majors—more than 19,000 men and women—will seek full-time jobs immediately after they graduate (Scheirer & Rogers, 1985; U.S. Department of Education, 1982). Psychology departments face many problems, but none is more pressing than the employability of their graduates. Forty-seven percent of the department chairpersons interviewed by telephone in the American Psychological Association's 1982 survey of undergraduate departments (APA, 1983) identified careers as a major issue for undergraduates in general and employment prospects for holders of psychology degrees in particular.

Traditionally, this is a thicket through which students must find their own way. Faculty members are seldom rewarded for advising undergraduates, especially about career options; often they are effectively penalized for spending time away from research and teaching. Rarely are they trained or evaluated for such advisement. The result is that many students go through their undergraduate programs with fair academic advisement and poor career advisement. Given this predicament, it may seem somewhat surprising that in 1984, of the psychology majors entering the labor force 1 year after graduation, 90% were employed. After 2 years, it was 94% (National Science Foundation, 1986).

Whether bright or average, students do not automatically know how to translate what they learn in the classroom into something that will be relevant to the workplace. McGovern (1979) reported that students without guidance had no sense of how to translate academic accomplishment into marketable skills, that they had no idea that business and industry are places in which to apply psychology, and that their typical aspiration was to become a psychotherapist. Two different assessments of career goals, he reported, revealed that psychology majors had little sense of how their coursework could help them in the workplace.

One career not open to the psychology graduate with a BA is that of psychologist. American psychology has clearly made the decision that the PhD, and occasionally the MA, is the entry-level qualification, and we cannot honestly speak of the BA in psychology as preparation for a career in psychology. It seldom is. Nevertheless, the "success stories" that follow in this introduction and several chapters in this volume do show that a bachelor's degree in psychology can lead to challenging and rewarding careers.

The liberal arts degree

The graduate with a BA or BS in psychology enters the job market indistinguishable from classmates who graduated with liberal arts degrees in English or sociology. Psychology graduates have to cope with the same economic realities faced by other liberal arts graduates: Jobs in psychology are as rare as jobs in literature or political science for the new baccalaureate. You should, however, be encouraged by this next observation. A liberal arts education is of great value in preparation both for work and for life. As you will read in chapter 4 of this book, most psychology graduates believe that the overall value of their BA in psychology has more to do with the general knowledge they gained through a liberal arts education than with specific applications of what they learned about psychology.

A recent study of more than 2,000 graduates of the University of Virginia (Benner & Hitchcock, 1986) identified the following five skills that these graduates regarded as critical to their current job success:

1. Oral communication—presenting one's ideas to others orally, both one-on-one and in groups.
2. Written communication—writing effective letters, reports, and other documents.
3. Interpersonal skills—understanding others' behavior and effectively dealing with others.
4. Problem solving skills—thinking and solving problems effectively.
5. Critical thinking—identify and analyzing problems, formulating and testing ideas.

More than 91% of the respondents in this study confirmed the value of a liberal arts education as the best preparation for their current careers. As one 1973 psychology graduate, now a banker earning $60,000 a year noted, "Liberal arts helped me to think and write." Furthermore, more than 33% of the respondents reported that their liberal arts degree gave them an advantage over others in their career area, and another 33% reported that they would have proceeded no differently in their careers had they pursued a more technical degree.

These results are in line with those of Kotter's 1982 study of general managers who manage a major division of large corporations. The major demands facing these general managers were to figure out what to do in a workplace characterized by uncertainty, great diversity, and an enormous quantity of relevant information. They had to get things done through people over whom they had little or no direct control. To meet these demands they needed to have excellent skills in communication, both oral and written, outstanding skills in interpersonal relations, and and exceptional skills in problem solving and critical thinking. They all had bachelor's degrees and had been student leaders in high school or college. Kotter concluded that these managers had early success that provided the foundation upon which to build further success. Chapter 6 will show you the skills and knowledge areas employers look for when hiring BAs. These kinds of results suggest that a successful liberal arts education, coupled with success as a student leader, can provide the necessary skills and background for later success in almost any career.

The argument that the liberal arts are a good preparation is further supported by a recent report from the National Science Foundation (1986) on 1983 bachelor's-degree graduates in psychology. The data reveal that 1 year after graduation 50% of these employed psychology majors were employed in business and industry and 27% were employed in science and engineering. An additional 15% were employed in educational institutions, 10% in nonprofit organizations, and 8% in federal, state, or local governments. The work that these graduates performed covered a broad range: 30% in management and administration, 28% in sales and professional services, 16% in teaching, and 12% in production and inspection. What can you do with a BA in psychology? As these data suggest, practically anything, once you take the initiative. And this book offers excellent information on an array of career avenues.

This is a big country, and whereas there are national labor market trends, the job market particular to a town or region is what really matters to the residents. So, especially if you stay in the area where you attended college after graduation, the local economy will matter more to you than broad and often vaguely defined national trends. However, to find out more about the occupational trends of psychology majors over the years, read chapter 12.

The psychology major

Few new baccalaureates can expect to find jobs in psychology without further training, although they do find many kinds of jobs. However, are these jobs related to psychology? Do formal coursework in psychology and extracurricular activities prepare students for these jobs? How are college experiences related to success and satisfaction in the workplace?

Looking at the prospects for liberal arts majors, do job market forecasters have anything useful or encouraging to tell psychology majors specifically? In 1984, the American Council on Education published a study entitled *Employment Prospects for College Graduates* (Henderson & Ottinger, 1984). Its major conclusions are as follows:

- A college degree is still a good investment.
- Job seekers are advised to research the job market, sharpen their communication skills, and get experience while still in college.
- The fastest growing occupations are predicted to be in health, engineering, and computer science.

Looking specifically at the prospects for college graduates in business, two major longitudinal studies conducted at AT&T (Howard, 1984) examined the relation between college experiences and management potential. According to these studies, college graduates were generally more successful as managers than were employees without college degrees. Measurable differences in abilities and moti-

vations account for this disparity. The undergraduate major was the strongest predictor of managerial performance and progress. Psychology majors were in the category of humanities and social science majors. This group had the best overall records, with particular strengths in interpersonal and verbal skills and motivation to advance; their one weakness was in quantitative ability. Business majors had the second best records, engineers and math and science majors, the worst (Howard, 1984).

Recent statistics indicate that employers are hiring more technically trained people and fewer liberal arts majors. The trend for college students to major in technical fields is a reaction to this pressure ("Facts in Brief," 1986). Most educators agree that this hiring trend is shortsighted; humanities and social science majors are excellent sources of general management talent, especially when they also have strong quantitative skills. The relevance to psychology majors is obvious.

James L. Ferguson, chair of General Foods Corporation, was recently cited as saying that the further an individual advances in the business world, the less important technical skills become. With more responsibility comes a greater need for flexibility, inventiveness, and the capacity to deal with people—skills that Ferguson associates with a broad liberal arts education ("Corporate Executive," 1985).

What are the specific skills developed by the psychology curriculum over and above those acquired from the liberal arts generally? A few psychology departments have attempted to analyze the kinds of skills their courses teach students and to match these with the demands of particular jobs and career paths. Virginia Commonwealth University conducted a major curriculum evaluation beginning in 1977 (McGovern & Ellett, 1980). Each faculty member was asked to identify for each course what students learn how to do in the course. How-to-do skills and then courses were grouped into categories of human relations and scientific research and writing. The seven human relations skills, for example, include how to do a formal interview and how to administer and score specific tests. The nine research and writing skills include how to collect and code data and how to make and record behavioral observations.

The next step was to match skills to job titles by doing basic occupational research using the *Dictionary of Occupational Titles* (U.S. Department of Labor, 1977) and job descriptions published by private business and industry, independent community service agencies, and government agencies at the federal, state, and local levels. The faculty researchers found 49 separate occupations that require a bachelor's degree as entry-level preparation. Common job titles for positions for which psychology majors were strong candidates included management trainee, personnel trainee, public relations and community representative, and sales representative.

The next step was to make practical use of this information in advising, by developing an undergraduate handbook that describes the faculty, the advising system, and educational and career planning. The handbook introduces the concept of "pathways" as a tool for planning a curriculum that leads to a definable career goal. For example, the pathway whose goal is employment in a personnel department includes taking courses in psychology, business administration, organizational behavior and management, and fieldwork at a corporation (McGovern & Ellett, 1980). Other pathways described are pre-health services, nursing, law, and three alternate pathways for graduate school in psychology. (Chapter 4 illustrates a similar system for taking on a minor or adding supplementary courses; chapter 5 offers advice on designing a career path to help you toward your career goal.)

Surveys designed to uncover what employers are looking for in terms of skill and knowledge are a related way to approach the task of career advising. At Virginia Commonwealth, faculty researched and interviewed employers as part of their work in designing career pathways for students. As part of a large national survey, business representatives rated the relative importance of 15 types of data used when choosing among job candidates. These business representatives gave highest ratings to personality, grades in major, and non-college jobs held. For a closer examination of these findings, look at chapter 6 of this book.

You may by now be thinking: "These data are all very interesting, but what do these studies and statistics mean to me? How do real students find first jobs that use skills learned as psychology majors? What is a career path? What are real employers looking for?" Let me offer a few specific examples. Richard Halgin recounts (Rogers, 1985) that in 1985 recruiters for Lord & Taylor Department Store, with no prodding from anyone, showed up on the University of Massachusetts at Amherst campus to recruit psychology students instead of management students. Why? Because they wanted trainees who understood human behavior rather than accounting. The following year Macy's recruited among both psychology and management students. These overtures from employers lead to jobs for psy-

chology majors. A peer counselor from one of the University of Massachusetts's advising programs was hired by a Macy's recruiter for a management trainee position, in part because of his experience in the peer counseling program.

A career development course at Creighton University led Sherry to discover a line of work she said she would otherwise never have imagined she would enjoy—through the process of doing informational interviews (Ware, interviewed in Rogers, 1985). She obtained a job with the state of Nebraska's work-release program, which involved caseworker-type responsibilities, working with and supervising individuals and groups, and doing some counseling. (See chapter 14 for advice on how to use informational interviewing to help you land a job.)

Mike, who found a job in private industry, is another success story. Mike was flying back to Omaha when he fell into conversation with the man seated next to him, who he soon discovered was a regional recruiter for a company that manufactures checks. Now Mike knew he was interested in some kind of entry-level business position in marketing, and he had learned never to pass up a contact (as chapters 2 and 5 will show). So after some casual conversation, he said he would be interested in learning more about this line of work. The man promised to put Mike in touch with the right person in Omaha. After several interviews Mike was offered an entry-level marketing position that could lead eventually to a district manager, supervisory position.

An example of a student successfully building her own career path is Corrine, who graduated with a BS in psychology and is now coordinator of orientation and pre-release services for the prison system in which she's been working (McGovern, interviewed in Rogers, 1985). Her first position at the corrections center was as a psychological test technician, and she credits her college Career Placement Center's testing course with giving her the basic skills for the position and getting her through the interviews. Corrine next worked as a counselor at the facility, taking additional workshops and seminars to learn about career counseling and group dynamics. In her current position she has taken on administrative responsibilities and sees herself as a manager of human resource development. (See chapter 7 for information on how to use the Career Placement Center.)

Jesse, also a psychology graduate with a BS, is successfully moving up a career path in personnel in a major private corporation (McGovern, interviewed in Rogers, 1985). Her first job with the company was as a job analyst. That job involved her in interviewing, hiring and promotion, affirmative action, and counseling employees. Her recent promotion to assistant personnel manager will mean more work in labor relations and safety. Looking back, Jesse identified as the most important aspects of her college preparation the experimental methods course and her fieldwork experience. The methods course disciplined her thinking and writing and taught her how to build an argument. Fieldwork introduced her to personnel work and to the corporation that hired her.

There are many new BA graduates who returned to school later in life, often after raising a family or to start a new career. Patricia Lunneborg of the University of Washington has taught a seminar on women and work (attended by students ranging in age from 20 to 65), which explores the processes of career development for women (Lunneborg, interviewed in Rogers, 1985). Donna was one student who took the seminar on women and work. At age 45 she returned to college to complete her bachelor's degree in psychology. She excelled academically and volunteered to work with elderly people. She enjoyed counseling so much that when a community police job opened up in her town she applied for it. One of 500 applicants for 2 positions, she was hired. For 2 years she held that job, using her psychology background and counseling experience in family dispute situations. Eventually she returned to counseling work with the elderly, but at a much higher level, thanks to her police experience.

There are two major conclusions to emphasize in these examples. First, psychology graduates are entering all kinds of occupations. The bachelor's degree in psychology is a flexible and versatile way to prepare for a career in diverse lines of work—you are not limited to human services. Second, psychology graduates are upwardly mobile, but their advancement is strongly correlated with training beyond the BA. Indeed, psychology baccalaureates are very likely to go on to graduate school in some field within a few years of completing their undergraduate degree.

A degree in psychology can provide you with tremendous flexibility in terms of your career direction in and out of the field of psychology. So, what are 40,000 psychology majors going to do next year? The bad news is that there is no simple career path set out for you. The good news is that your degree can lead to a variety of worthwhile and exciting careers. It is up to you to decide what direction to take. This book can help you.

References

American Psychological Association. (1983). *Results: Phase 1 survey of undergraduate department chairs.* Washington, DC: Author.

Benner, R. S., & Hitchcock, S. T. (1986). *Life after liberal arts.* Charlottesville: University of Virginia.

Corporate executive calls for educational reforms. (1985, November 11). Higher Education and National Affairs, pp. 1, 6.

Facts in brief. (1986, January 27). Higher Education and National Affairs, p. 3.

Henderson C., & Ottinger, C. (1984). Employment prospects for college graduates. ACE Policy Brief. Washington, DC: American Council on Education.

Howard, A. (1984). *College experiences and managerial performance: Report to management.* New York: AT&T.

Kotter, J. P. (1982). *The general managers.* New York: Free Press.

McGovern, T. V. (1979). Development of a career planning program for undergraduate psychology majors. *Teaching of Psychology, 6,* 183-184.

McGovern, T. V., & Ellett, S. E. (1980). Bridging the gap: Psychology classroom to the marketplace. *Teaching of Psychology, 7,* 237-238.

National Science Foundation. (1986). *Characteristics of recent science/engineering graduates: 1984.* Washington, DC: Author.

Rogers, A. M. (1985, December). [Interviews with Richard P. Halgin, University of Massachusetts at Amherst; Patricia W. Lunneborg, University of Washington; Thomas V. McGovern, Virginia Commonwealth University; and Mark Ware, Creighton University]. Paper presented at the Eighth National Institute on Teaching of Psychology, Clearwater, FL.

Scheirer, C. J., & Rogers, A. M. (1985). *The undergraduate psychology curriculum.* Washington, DC: American Psychological Association.

U.S. Department of Education, National Center for Education Statistics. (1982). *Earned degrees conferred, 1980-81 and 1981-82.* Washington, DC: Author.

U.S. Department of Labor, Employment and Training Administration. (1977). *Dictionary of occupational titles* (4th ed.). Washington, DC: U.S. Government Printing Office.

Dr. Goodstein gratefully acknowledges the help of Vivian Makosky and Anne Rogers of the APA Office of Educational Affairs in the preparation of this introduction. The entire speech, originally presented at the 1986 APA Convention, is printed in the *Psi Chi Newsletter* (Winter 1987).

PART 1

Is psychology for you?

Chapter 1

Psychology, your major, and you

Perhaps you are in college and have yet to decide upon a major. Perhaps you have a good idea about what you want to do, but are still considering your options. Perhaps you have already decided on and declared a major, yet you feel the need for some additional guidance or information. Or perhaps you are finishing your degree and would like some advice about what to do next.

Whatever your circumstances, you may have questions on your mind about whether there is a place for psychology in your future. This book is intended to help answer these questions and to facilitate your choice of a major, a degree, or a career path. Whether or not you choose to major in psychology, this book can be useful. Many of its precepts can be applied to any field and can enable you to make more informed decisions about courses to take, majors to consider, and career to pursue.

By reading this book, you are already putting some effort into decision making. It is vital for you to take the initiative in planning your future. Any decision about majors or careers is ultimately yours to make. Parents, friends, or professors may act as sounding boards, but they should not make the decisions for you.

There are right and wrong reasons for choosing a major or a career. The right reasons include interest, commitment, and satisfaction. The wrong reasons include almost everything else. Many students choose whatever major seems to provide the best job prospects at a particular time, regardless of whether they have an aptitude for or an interest in that field. Keep in mind that the decisions you make now will have a tremendous impact on the course of your life. Spending time, effort, and money preparing for a career in which you have little or no interest or aptitude may become a problem later on.

Now is the time for you not only to think about a major field of study, but also to begin

Material for this chapter was contributed in part by Paula Sachs Wise, Western Illinois University. Descriptions of what psychologists do were taken from Careers in Psychology *(see full bibliographic listing in chapter 23).*

taking the necessary steps to complete your major successfully. This book is designed to help guide you through the process.

What do psychologists do?

Psychology is the study of behavior, human as well as animal. Psychologists are individuals with advanced training who study behavior and apply their knowledge and skills in a variety of ways.

For example, some psychologists are employed

• as teachers—psychologists teach classes in psychology at universities, four-year and two-year colleges, and high schools;
• as researchers—psychologists are employed by universities, government agencies, the military, and businesses to conduct basic and applied studies of human behavior;
• as service providers—psychologists work with people of all ages and backgrounds who are coping with every imaginable kind of problem, by assessing their needs and providing appropriate treatment;
• as administrators—psychologists work as managers in hospitals, mental health clinics, nonprofit organizations, government agencies, schools, universities, and businesses; and
• as consultants—psychologists with expertise in a variety of areas are hired by organizations to provide consultative services on a subject or problem in which the consultant is an expert. These services can include designing a marketing survey, organizing outpatient mental health services for adolescents, or working with teachers to facilitate children's learning and mental health.

Psychologists frequently perform in more than one of these roles. For example, a psychologist might teach graduate students at a university and also maintain a private practice providing therapy to individual clients, families, or groups. In addition to teaching, psychologist-researchers frequently provide consultative services to organizations or individuals. A person with a background in psychology has many career paths from which to choose. Your potential career options will depend upon your level of training and your choice of a particular area in which to concentrate.

Whether you are interested in human services, computers, management, education, high technology, sports, or many other fields, you are likely to find psychologists working in that field. When you remember that psychology involves the study of behavior, it is not surprising to find such a vast array of applications.

There is great flexibility and diversity within psychology. Following are brief summaries of some of the major specialty areas within psychology which you can pursue. You should view these as opportunities, not limitations, because new areas are constantly emerging.

Information about specific areas of psychology can be obtained from relevant APA Divisions (see chapter 23). Other ways to become informed are to read relevant articles in journals and books, write to colleges and universities with specialized training programs, and talk to psychologists knowledgeable about the area.

Clinical psychology. Clinical psychologists assess and treat people with problems. Such problems may range from the "normal" psychological crises related to biological growth (e.g., rebellion in adolescence) to less common conditions such as schizophrenia or depression. Many clinical psychologists also conduct research. For example, they may study the characteristics of psychotherapists associated with patient improvements, or they may investigate the factors that relate to high self esteem, or to the development of schizophrenia.

Clinical psychologists work in academic institutions and health care settings such as clinics, hospitals, community mental health centers, or private practice. Some clinical psychologists focus their interests on special populations such as children, minority group members, or the elderly. Others specialize in the treatment of certain types of problems such as phobias, eating disorders, or depression. Still others prefer to work as generalists, working with all ages and problems rather than restricting their practice. Opportunities in clinical psychology are expanding to populations that have not been adequately served in the past such as the elderly, prison inmates, and the poor.

In most states people with master's and bachelor's degrees may not practice psychology independently. They may, however, perform the whole gamut of psychological services in clinical settings under the supervision of doctoral-level psychologists.

Community psychology. Community psychologists are concerned with behavior in natural settings—the home, the neighborhood, and the workplace. They seek to identify factors that contribute to normal and abnormal behavior in these settings. Community psychologists also emphasize the importance of preventing problems before they occur. Whereas clinical psychologists tend to focus on individuals who show signs of a disorder, many community psychologists concentrate their efforts either on groups of people who may be at risk for developing difficulties or on the population in general.

Counseling psychology. Counseling psychologists foster and improve normal human functioning across the life span by helping people solve problems, make decisions, and cope with the stresses of everyday life. Typically, counseling psychologists work with people who are having difficulties coping with a particular event or aspect of their lives. They work with clients individually or in groups, assessing their needs and providing a variety of therapies, ranging from behavior modification to interpersonally oriented approaches.

Counseling psychologists often use research to evaluate the effectiveness of treatments and to search for novel approaches to assessing problems and changing behavior. Research methods may include structured tests, interviews, interest inventories, and observations. They also may be involved in a variety of activities such as helping people to stop smoking or to adjust to college, consulting on physical problems that might have psychological causes or be responsive to treatment with psychological techniques, teaching graduate-level practica in counseling, or developing and testing techniques that students can use to reduce their anxiety about taking examinations.

Many counseling psychologists work in academic settings, but an increasing number are being employed in health care institutions, such as community mental health centers, Veterans Administration hospitals, and private clinics. Those with master's degrees are often found in educational institutions, clinics, business, industry, government, and other human service agencies.

Developmental psychology. Developmental psychologists study human development across the life span, from newborn to aged. Developmental psychologists are interested in the description, measurement, and explanation of age-related changes in behavior; stages of emotional development; universal traits and individual differences; and abnormal changes in development.

Many doctoral-level developmental psychologists are employed in academic settings, teaching and doing research. They often consult on programs in day-care centers, preschools, and hospitals and clinics for children. They also evaluate intervention programs such as Head Start and Follow Through and provide other direct services to children and families. Other developmental psychologists focus their attention on problems of aging and work in programs targeted at older populations. Per-

sons with bachelor's- and master's-level training in developmental psychology work in applied settings such as day-care centers and in programs with youth groups.

Educational psychology. Educational psychologists study how people learn, and they design the methods and materials used to educate people of all ages. Many educational psychologists work in universities, in both psychology departments and schools of education. Some conduct basic research on topics related to the learning of reading, writing, mathematics, and science. Others develop new methods of instruction including designing computer software. Still others train teachers and they investigate factors that affect teachers' performance and morale. Educational psychologists conduct research in schools and in federal, state, and local education agencies. They may be employed by governmental agencies or the corporate sector to analyze employees' skills and to design and implement training programs.

Traditionally, job opportunities for educational psychologists have been concentrated in academic and educational settings and have been limited to those with doctoral degrees. Recently industry and the military are offering increased possibilities for people with doctoral degrees who can design and evaluate systems to teach complex technical skills. There are new opportunities in evaluation of social problems and policies as well. All of these areas may begin to provide jobs for those with master's degrees.

Environmental psychology. Environmental psychologists are concerned with the relations between psychological processes and physical environments. These environments range from homes and offices to urban areas and regions. Environmental psychologists may do basic research, for example, on people's attitudes toward different environments or their sense of personal space. Or their research may be applied, such as evaluating an office design or assessing the psychological impact of a government's plan to build a new waste-treatment plant.

Experimental psychology. "Experimental psychologist" is a general title applied to a diverse group of psychologists who conduct research on and often teach about a variety of basic behavioral processes. These processes include learning; sensation; perception; human performance; motivation; memory; language, thinking, and communication; and the physiological processes underlying behaviors such as eating, reading, and problem solving. Experimental psychologists study the basic processes by which humans take in, store, retrieve, express, and apply knowledge. They also study the behavior of animals, often with a view to gaining a better understanding of human behavior, but sometimes also because it is intrinsically interesting.

Most experimental psychologists work in academic settings, teaching courses and supervising students' research in addition to conducting their own research. Experimental psychologists are also employed by research institutions, business, industry, and government. A research-oriented doctoral degree is usually needed for advancement and mobility in experimental psychology.

Industrial/organizational psychology. Industrial/organizational psychologists are concerned with the relation between people and work. Their interests include organizational structure and organizational change; workers' productivity and job satisfaction; consumer behavior; selection, placement, training, and development of personnel; and the interaction between humans and machines. Their responsibilities on the job include research, development (translating the results of research into usable products or procedures), and problem solving.

Industrial/organizational psychologists work in businesses, industries, governments, and colleges and universities. Some may be self-employed as consultants or work for management consulting firms. In a business, industry, or government setting, industrial/organizational psychologists might study the procedures on an assembly line and suggest changes to reduce the monotony and increase the responsibility of workers. Or they might advise management on how to develop programs to identify staff with management potential or administer a counseling service for employees on career development and preparation for retirement.

Consumer psychologists are industrial/organizational psychologists whose interests lie in consumers' reactions to a company's products or services. They investigate consumers' preferences for a particular package design or television commercial, for example, and develop strategies for marketing products. They also try to improve the acceptability and the safety of products and to help the consumer make better decisions.

Engineering psychologists are industrial/organizational psychologists concerned with improving the interaction between humans and their working environments, including jobs and the contexts in which they are performed. Engineering psychologists help design systems that require people and machines to interact,

such as video-display units; they may also develop aids for training people to use those systems.

Personnel psychologists are industrial/organizational psychologists who develop and validate procedures to select and evaluate personnel. They may, for example, develop instruments and guides for interviewers to use in screening applicants for positions, or they may work with management and union representatives to develop criteria for assessing employees' performance.

Jobs for industrial/organizational psychologists are available at both the master's and the doctoral level. Opportunities for those with master's degrees tend to be concentrated in business, industry, and government settings; doctoral-level psychologists also work in academic settings and independent consulting work.

Neuropsychology and psychobiology. Psychobiologists and neuropsychologists investigate the relation between physical systems and behavior. Topics they study include the relation of specific biochemical mechanisms in the brain to behavior, the relation of brain structure to function, and the chemical and physical changes that occur in the body when we experience different emotions. Neuropsychologists also diagnose and treat disorders related to the central nervous system. They may diagnose behavioral disturbances related to suspected dysfunctions of the central nervous system and treat patients by teaching them new ways to acquire and process information—a technique known as cognitive retraining.

Clinical neuropsychologists work in the neurology, neurosurgery, psychiatric, and pediatric units of hospitals, and in clinics. They also work in academic settings where they conduct research and train other neuropsychologists, clinical psychologists, and medical doctors. Most positions in neuropsychology and biopsychology are at the doctoral level, and many require postdoctoral training. Limited opportunities exist at the bachelor's and master's level for technicians and research assistants.

Psychometrics and quantitative psychology. Psychometric and quantitative psychologists are concerned with the methods and techniques used in acquiring and applying psychological knowledge. A psychometrician may revise old intelligence, personality, and aptitude tests or devise new ones. These tests might be used in clinical, counseling, and school settings, and in business and industry. Other quantitative psychologists might assist a researcher in psychology or in another field design or interpret the results of an experiment. To accomplish these tasks, they may design new techniques for analyzing information.

Psychometricians and quantitative psychologists typically are well trained in mathematics, statistics, and computer programming and technology. Doctoral-level psychometricians and quantitative psychologists are employed mainly by universities and colleges, testing companies, private research firms, and government agencies. Those with master's degrees often work for testing companies and private research firms.

Rehabilitation psychology. Rehabilitation psychologists are researchers and practitioners who work with people who have suffered a physical deprivation or loss, either at birth or through later damage such as resulting from a stroke. They sometimes help people adjust to the physical handicaps associated with aging. Typically, people treated by rehabilitation psychologists face both psychological and situational barriers to effective functioning in the world.

Many rehabilitation psychologists work in medical rehabilitation institutes and hospitals. Other rehabilitation psychologists work in medical schools and universities, serve as consultants to or as administrators in state and federal vocational rehabilitation agencies, or have private practices serving people who have disabilities.

School psychology. School psychologists are concerned with the intellectual, educational, social, and emotional development of children. They are also concerned with creating environments that facilitate learning and mental health. They may evaluate and plan programs for children with special needs or deal with less severe problems such as disruptive behavior in the classroom. They sometimes engage in program development and staff consultation to prevent problems. Occasionally, they provide assistance to teachers in classroom management, consult with parents and teachers on ways to support a child's efforts in school, and consult with school administrators on a variety of psychological and educational issues.

School psychologists may also be found at universities, where they train students to become school psychologists and they conduct research (e.g., comparing the effectiveness of different tests in diagnosing a child's learning problems). Some school psychologists work in private practice. To be employed as a school

psychologist of a given state, you must have completed a training program approved by the state in which you wish to work and be certified by the state. Many states require school psychologists to have a master's degree or a minimum of 60 semester hours of coursework to become certified.

School psychologists trained at the doctoral level are usually employed in school settings or in university training programs. In school settings, doctoral-level school psychologists often perform administrative and supervisory services. Typically, in comparison to nondoctoral professionals in school psychology, the doctoral-level school psychologist has more research and evaluation training as well as more in-depth clinical and consultative training. The number of jobs in school psychology has increased slowly but steadily in the last decade. The opportunities vary from state to state but are generally quite favorable.

Social psychology. Social psychologists study how people interact with each other and how they are affected by their social environments. They study individuals as well as groups, observable behaviors, and private thoughts. Topics of interest to social psychologists include personality theories, the formation of attitudes and attitude change, attractions between people such as friendship and love, prejudice, group dynamics, and violence and aggression. Social psychologists might, for example, study how attitudes toward the elderly influence the elderly person's self-concept, or they might investigate how unwritten rules of behavior develop in groups and how those rules regulate the conduct of group members.

Social psychologists can be found in a wide variety of academic settings, and, increasingly, in many nonacademic settings. For example, more social psychologists than before now work in advertising agencies, corporations, hospitals, educational institutions, and architectural and engineering firms as researchers, consultants, and personnel managers. As with experimental psychology, a research-oriented doctoral degree is usually necessary in social psychology.

Psychologists also use their degrees as a foundation for careers in related fields such as business or law. Furthermore, there are numerous areas of psychology that are either emerging or expanding, or might be considered unconventional. These applications of psychology are described in Part 3 of this book.

Chapter 2

How to decide on a major

In career decision making, people typically go through a process of gathering information and mulling it over before making a choice. It is a process that usually involves a succession of stages: People proceed from the *exploration* stage to the *crystallization* stage, to the *choice* stage, and finally to the *clarification* stage. This process doesn't follow a straight line and isn't necessarily rational or even conscious. However, it can be so frightening that people would rather put it off.

If you are just beginning the process of deciding your major, you will probably explore and crystallize (or more clearly define) your goals for about 2 years before you choose a major and clarify that choice. Most students select their major in their junior year, after much weighing and rejecting of alternatives. Read this chapter and see where you are in the process. To aid in clarifying your goals while you are in college, do the Other Students' Exercise. Do the Choice Exercise that follows to record your decision. This exercise is handy to show to parents, spouses, and friends who ask, "Why are you majoring in psychology?"

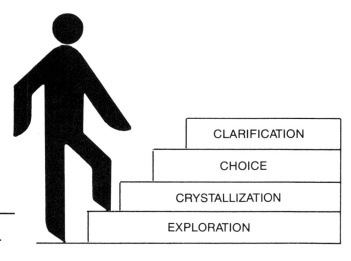

Material for this chapter was contributed by Patricia W. Lunneborg, University of Washington.

The exploration and crystallization stages

College is your first big step on the road to your future. So from the start take advantage of all the resources around you. The following are steps you should take to help you decide what you really want to do. Check off those you have already done. Begin those you have not. You may not be able to complete every step during your college years, but remember, the more you can accomplish, the further ahead you will be.

• *Gather information about careers.* Every college has career resource centers with names like Career Placement Center, Advising Office, or Occupational Library. Visit them all. Read the notices on their bulletin boards. Pick up every free pamphlet or booklet you can find. Talk with anyone who is available. Keep a notebook devoted solely to your career material and notes. Also visit various department offices, such as the English, art, mathematics, and psychology departments and offices in the professional schools, such as business, engineering, and education. Read their pamphlet literature and talk to their staff as part of your information gathering.

• *Take a variety of courses.* You can't rush exploration. You simply have to be patient with and proud of yourself as you take courses that help you learn what interests you. Remember to consider noncredit courses as well, which may be taught by nonacademic people and in nonacademic settings.

• *Do some fieldwork.* Whether for credit or not, volunteer work and internships help you to crystallize tentative choices made through reading and academic study. You must test your impressions of what really goes on in that field—get to know the world of work.

• *Take part in extracurricular activities.* Participation in intramural sports, student government, community service organizations, and student clubs will help you develop leadership skills, teamwork abilities, breadth, self-confidence, and initiative, all of which lead to knowing more about yourself.

• *Get paid work experience.* Don't lament working while going to school. Employers prefer students who worked their way through college!

• *Talk to people.* Everyone you meet (instructors, other students, co-workers, the person sitting next to you on the bus, the couple ahead of you in line) can potentially teach you something valuable for your career decision making. Don't hesitate to ask questions such

as "What's it like working there? What do you like about your job? How are things in your field right now?"

• *Get to know your interests, values, and aptitudes.* Sign up for individual or group career guidance at your Career Placement Center. Such sessions usually involve taking tests and taking part in interpreting them. Read chapter 6 of this book for further details. Also, your college bookstore has dozens of self-help books if you prefer to do this assessment alone.

• *Prepare a résumé and keep it up to date.* You should always have a résumé, if for no other reason than to look at when you get downhearted and wonder just who you are, anyway! Your interests, work-related values, and proven abilities can be stated there. If that sounds too threatening, then do a straightforward work history. Write down everything you have ever done, such as part-time jobs, summer jobs, or volunteer work. Give the name and address of each employer, your job title, your duties, and the dates you worked there. For specific examples, read chapters 12 and 13 of this book.

• *Read books like this one.* This book has information to help you decide whether psychology is the major, as well as career, for you. The following chapters list jobs that psychology baccalaureates hold, skills that employers value in psychology graduates, where to look for jobs in psychology, and how to get ready for graduate school. What other books do advisors on your campus recommend?

By taking advantage of the resources at hand, you can effectively explore your course and career options. The process of crystallizing is realizing what it is you really want to do. To help you with this exploration, try the Other Students' Exercise.

The Other Students' Exercise

Step 1. Go through the following list and check the three learning goals that you think other students have. Think of other students you know and why you think they're in college. How do you believe they would finish the sentence, "I really want to learn. . . ."?

I REALLY WANT TO LEARN . . .

—— How to be more creative

—— How to change society

—— How to continue to learn

—— How to state hypotheses and test them

—— How to think logically

—— How to write well

—— How to speak effectively to others

—— How to be more confident socially

—— More about the arts

—— More about myself

—— More about values and ideas

—— New fields of knowledge

—— New modes of problem solving

—— Practical skills and knowledge

—— How to get along with all kinds of people

—— The background necessary for a particular career

—— How to appreciate my own and other cultures

Step 2. Now pick the learning goal that you value most of other students and write it below as your top learning goal. This goal my be derived from one of the learning goals you checked off above or it could be unrelated.

MY TOP LEARNING GOAL IS

_____

Step 3. Now list the concrete steps you can take to reach it during the next year.

THREE ACTIONS I CAN TAKE TO REACH THIS GOAL:

1. Take courses in

_____, _____, _____, and _____.

2. Join this extracurricular activity

_____

_____

3. Do volunteer work at

_____

_____

The choice stage

When you reach the choice stage, you will probably have experienced a change in outlook. You will feel more certain about the kind of work you want to do and clearer about the major you want to pursue. You should have a clearer idea of what your requirements are and what is left to be done. If you feel that you are at this stage, try the following exercise. This exercise provides a scale that you can look at in order to judge the value of various majors to you. Through it, you can choose your college major.

The Choice Exercise

Step 1. Ask yourself the following questions and rate the likelihood of each. Are my chances of . . . poor, good, or very good?

1. Being accepted into the major _____

2. Making the grades necessary to graduate _____

3. Making the grades required for graduate study in the major _____

If you are able to answer "very good" to the first two of these questions for any majors you are considering, go to Step 2 and evaluate and compare the majors by using the following rating scheme.

Step 2. For any major you are considering, rate the following factors in terms of their importance to you, using this scale: 1 = no importance, 2 = some importance, 3 = moderate importance, 4 = great importance.

Factors	Rate
Good bachelor's-level job prospects	_____
Available career-oriented departmental advising	_____
Good contacts and relations between faculty and community	_____
Good general background for any career	_____
Good skills training for any career	_____
Good graduate-level job prospects	_____
Available independent study opportunities	_____
Available job-related fieldwork	_____
Major close to my career interests	_____
Good department reputation	_____
Highly interesting subject matter	_____

Step 3. You may want to use the following exercise several times while you are choosing a major. Use it to evaluate psychology or any other major you are considering. Write in the majors you are considering.

_____ Psychology _____

_____ _____

_____ _____

_____ _____

Now, how do you believe these majors rate at your college?
Using the same factors as in Step 2, rate these majors, using the same point scale as before:
1 = none, 2 = some, 3 = moderate, 4 = great.
Enter these points in column A. Then multiply the amount of each factor by the corresponding importance value that you provided in Step 2 (column B). Complete the following table for each major being evaluated.

Column A Rating of major	Column B Your importance values from Step 2	Column C Multiply columns A and B
_____ Good bachelor's-level job prospects	_____	_____
_____ Available career-oriented departmental advising	_____	_____
_____ Good contacts and relations between faculty and community	_____	_____
_____ Good general background for any career	_____	_____
_____ Good skills training for any career	_____	_____
_____ Good graduate-level job prospects	_____	_____
_____ Available independent study opportunities	_____	_____
_____ Available job-related fieldwork	_____	_____
_____ Major close to my career interests	_____	_____
_____ Good department reputation	_____	_____
_____ Highly interesting subject matter	_____	_____
_____	SUM	_____

What's the sum of these multiplied values? Add up column C to find out.
Compare the various majors. The highest score wins!

The clarification stage

Once you have chosen a major, you must clarify that choice and your career direction. If you choose psychology as your major, you must ask yourself which of the following will be your primary focus? Which might be your alternate goal?

- A career requiring a bachelor's degree, related to psychology
- A career requiring a bachelor's degree, not related to psychology
- A career requiring graduate study in psychology
- A career requiring graduate study in another area

For both bachelor's-level plans, you should clarify what supplementary areas of study to choose. The possibilities are numerous, including business administration, communications, economics, English, health, sociology, urban planning, wildlife science, and so forth. Minoring or taking a concentration of courses in a particular area of study can greatly strengthen your degree. This book offers a wealth of information about supplementary areas of study (read specifically chapters 4, 5, and 8).

For a career that requires graduate study in psychology, this book contains a great deal you need to know about what should go into a competitive undergraduate record (see chapter 15). For law school (see chapter 10), medical school, business administration, librarianship, hospital administration, public affairs careers, and so forth, you can determine from appropriate resources and advisors what supplementary work you may need. Also, this book contains relevant information. Read on!

Chapter 3

Selecting psychology as your college major

Before you decide to major in psychology, ask yourself whether this is really what you want to do with regard to your own development, education, and career. What are your true interests and ambitions? Are they compatible with psychology? Answering the following questions may help you to define your interests and goals.

- Why should I major in psychology?
- Is it the right decision for me?
- What options are available for psychology majors?
- Am I willing to attend graduate school to attain my goals?
- What would I like to be doing 5, 10, and 25 years after I graduate?
- What are my strengths and weaknesses? Likes and dislikes?
- How committed am I to learning about prospective careers?
- Am I willing to do volunteer work or field work?

Of course, there are no right or wrong answers to these questions. But they do provide an initial step in personal career planning and in getting to know yourself.

Often students say that they are interested in majoring in psychology because they want to be psychologists. If this is what you want, be aware that to be a psychologist, you are required to complete 5 to 9 years of graduate study. A practicing psychologist usually holds a doctoral degree, must meet proper accreditation standards, and must pass state and local licensing exams. Receiving a bachelor's degree in psychology, no matter how extensive your undergraduate education, does not entitle you to be called a psychologist.

Students also say they are interested in psychology because they want to help people. If this is your wish, you do not necessarily need

Material for this chapter was contributed by Bernardo J. Carducci, Indiana University Southeast; Richard M. Suinn, Colorado State University; and Paula Sachs Wise, Western Illinois University.

a psychology degree. Therapists, counselors, clergy men and women, social workers, psychiatric assistants, nursing aides, and hospital orderlies are a few of the many besides psychologists who help people. Some of these other individuals may have training in psychology, but their jobs usually do not require such training. The point is that there are many individuals who are not psychologists who do help people. The nature of the problems they treat varies, as does the nature of their professional training.

If you want to help people, ask yourself what types of problems you want to help people solve. It could be that the best training for you might be in a discipline other than psychology. However, a psychology major may be precisely the training you need to meet your immediate and long-term objectives.

So, should you become a psychology major? Yes, if you want to help people; and if you are willing to undertake an orderly, scientific approach to understanding the sometimes irrational nature of human behavior; and if you are willing to invest a great deal of time and effort in your studies.

It is important for you to consider the benefits of having a bachelor's degree in psychology. A bachelor's degree in psychology can open a whole world of professional opportunities, such as

- sales
- personnel
- management training
- public relations
- research
- technical writing
- advertising
- computer programming
- psychological services
- child care
- teaching
- vocational training

Remember that psychology involves the study of behavior. As a result, wherever you work with people, knowledge of psychology should make it possible for you to work more effectively with them. The knowledge you acquire in psychology can be put to work in a variety of employment settings. The key is recognizing how, when, and where psychology can be applied. This book will begin to show you the possibilities.

How to decide whether psychology is for you

The following suggestions may help you determine whether psychology is the right major for you.

Keep informed of all of the undergraduate degree programs offered at your college or university. Read through the college bulletin or catalog to see the various course offerings for all degree programs, including those for psychology. See what interests you. Find out what courses outside a particular major are required for a bachelor's degree. Most psychology programs, for instance, require you to take courses in math or statistics. Make sure you know what is expected of you and what your options are before you choose any particular degree path.

Talk to individuals in various professions. If you have an idea of what you want to do after college, talk to people in that particular field. Ask them what they consider valuable training for their jobs. They may recommend not only courses to take but also extracurricular activities, internships, or volunteer work that would be beneficial. Such experiences may help you decide what you like and dislike and point you in a more focused direction.

Familiarize yourself with the services of the Career Placement Center on your campus. Talk to the counselors there and use the Center's resources. The earlier you visit the Center in your college career, the more informed you will be about your occupational and professional career alternatives, and the sooner you will be able to start formulating a career-development strategy. Read chapter 7 for a more detailed explanation about using your Career Placement Center.

Whether you decide to pursue the rigors of graduate school or find employment upon graduating, it is important for you to consider the choice of your major as a career decision. What you choose to do now will have a bearing on your future. It is more important that you choose what interests you most. It is a waste of time, effort, and money for you to choose a major you do not enjoy, cannot understand, or find uninteresting.

A degree in psychology can lead to many opportunities. This book can help you recognize some of these opportunities so that you may apply your knowledge and skills and benefit from them. On the other hand, this book cannot give you all the answers to your questions, nor can it make the decision for you. A careful reading of this book can point you in the right direction and provide you with information about psychology as a major. You must decide whether psychology is the major for you.

Chapter 4

Life as a psychology major

Once you have chosen psychology as your major, you will need to plan your college career in greater detail and with greater focus. You will probably ask yourself, "How do I go complete a major in psychology?" Even while tackling the rigors of your psychology curriculum, you will be getting a liberal arts education. A *liberal arts* education is intended to provide general knowledge and to develop general intellectual capacities, reason, and judgment. The purpose of a liberal arts education is not to prepare you for a job but to cultivate and enrich you mentally, morally, and aesthetically; to teach you to think critically; and to make you a free and responsible citizen.

The idea is an ancient and noble one. In a traditional sense, the term liberal arts education extends to the curricula of liberal arts colleges. Such curricula emphasize philosophy rather than technique, principles rather than application, culture rather than career, breadth rather than narrowness (Kulik, 1973). Inasmuch as your occupational preparation will require you to narrow your focus and choices, your college education should allow you to broaden your horizons. A liberal arts education is meant to open the mind and give you a better understanding of the world and to make you a well-rounded individual. In short, a liberal arts education prepares you to be a generalist rather than a specialist. Although such an education won't specifically prepare you to be a doctor, engineer, or accountant, it nevertheless can help you to advance in business, school, and life.

No doubt you have already encountered a traditional aspect of the liberal arts in a practical sense. Course requirements set down by the college itself, not individual departments, are a standard part of a liberal arts curriculum. These core course requirements will introduce you to various areas of study and will broaden your knowledge. You may find it beneficial to view your eventual bachelor's degree

Material for this chapter was contributed or adapted by Charles S. Wilkinson. The survey on how psychology graduates feel about their degrees was conducted and reported by Patricia W. Lunneborg, University of Washington, and Vicki M. Wilson, Hospital Commission, Olympia, WA.

in psychology as a liberal arts degree that is supported by a range of subjects and knowledge. Most students unfortunately prefer to view a bachelor's degree as specialized knowhow; however, a mere bachelor's degree does not confer the status of philosopher, historian, sociologist, or psychologist. Specialization with a bachelor's degree consists of general organizational and interpersonal knowledge. For instance, an understanding of human behavior is relevant to any occupation or situation involving interaction with others.

Joining the psychology department

Getting to know your school's psychology department should be the first step in pursuing your major. You may be spending a lot of time in the psychology building or department or advisor's office. Talk to the staff who work there and get to know the whereabouts of various resources. Many departments have student lounges or information offices. Visit them and read available handouts or material on their bulletin boards. In short, make this place your home away from home.

You must refer to your college catalog for explanations of department course requirements. Seek additional information from department faculty or an advisor. As a psychology major you should be aware of the structure and specific requirements of your program in order to take full advantage of your scheduling from semester to semester. Specific course requirements and individual course names differ somewhat from college to college, but general requirements are much the same for all psychology programs.

Also, determine the courses outside the psychology department that are required by the degree program. These requirements are usually in addition to the general core college requirements. For instance, you may be required to take courses in related areas, such as in economics, geography, or sociology. Statistics or a math equivalent is almost always required for a psychology degree.

Within the department's course lists will be an array of requirements and options. Many of these are not specific courses but areas of concentration in psychology, such as experimental, social/personality, clinical, and developmental. Other specialized areas may include history and systems or industrial/organizational or educational psychology.

Fundamental to your degree, and a usual requirement for all prospective psychology majors, is introductory psychology, the prerequisite for all other psychology courses. The goal of this introductory course is to convey elementary concepts and facts of the discipline, introduce the full range of its subject matter, express its basic attitudes, present its newest findings, and provide some guidelines for further studies. How this goal is achieved depends on the college—whether introductory is one semester or two, the extent of lab work, and so forth—yet reflects the orientation of the particular psychology department.

The most common major is general psychology, although many students choose specialized ones such as industrial/organizational or educational. You usually need 9 to 12 courses (27 to 36 credit hours) to graduate with a major in psychology.

Although most psychology departments require only classroom and lab work for the bachelor's degree, occasionally fieldwork or an internship may also be required. Often such hands-on experience can be chosen as an elective. As you will read in subsequent chapters, fieldwork and internship experience can be quite valuable if and when you seek employment or apply to graduate school.

The added value of having a minor

When planning your degree, you might consider selecting a minor to complement your psychology major. Having completed a minor in business administration, marketing, or journalism, for instance, could enhance your job prospects (for specific information on psychology and business, see chapter 8.) A minor can have other advantages as well. It can fill gaps in your course scheduling by providing an additional track or set of courses for you to complete. A minor also looks impressive, as if you had wisely and diligently spent your college time and were serious about your studies. More importantly, however, a minor provides you with additional knowledge. The requirements for a minor are usually half of those for a major (18 credit hours versus 36). Usually 6 to 9 credit hours must be in advanced level courses. Selecting a minor field can sometimes be difficult. To help you decide, the following are factors to consider (adapted from Holloway, 1985).

Employability. If you are concerned primarily about your future job prospects, select a minor that is marketable. Fields you may wish to consider are

- business administration
- economics
- computer science
- journalism
- technical writing
- criminal justice
- marketing

Consult with faculty in these departments for additional information about employment potential and coursework.

A related field. You may wish to choose a field related to psychology. Because psychology is concerned with human and animal behavior, a minor that pertains to more specific kinds of behavior or more specific populations can provide a more comprehensive picture. Examples include

- sociology
- anthropology
- child development
- rehabilitation
- social work
- employee relations
- special education
- counseling
- communications

Such fields can also be marketable for professional entry-level positions.

Preparation for graduate school. Virtually all graduate school programs require core courses in advanced statistics, experimental design, and other quantitative coursework. Graduate students are required to conduct research projects through coursework, research practica, theses, dissertations, and fellowships or assistantships. Also, many specialties require written or orally presented case reports associated with internship experience. Minors that would help to prepare you for these graduate requirements include

- English
- technical writing
- computer science
- mathematics
- public speaking
- communications

Another avenue you might choose is the double major, which can favorably impress graduate schools and employers. Extensive planning and preparation is required, however, and you should probably make your decision to double-major before your sophomore year. Several psychology programs, however, allow only second majors that are associated with or fit in with the psychology program. Check with your advisor before proceeding.

Consulting your faculty advisor about your master plan

As an initial step in planning your degree program, talk with your faculty advisor. However, you should do some basic preparation before your initial meeting. Begin by gathering and studying information about college and major requirements and programs in your college catalog or material from particular departments. Prepare questions based on your needs and what you think you want to do. As you talk with your advisor, check off items as they are covered and take notes about courses, further work needed, and sources of information.

Although this initial meeting should center on your degree requirements and concerns, it is also a time to begin discussing your post-graduation plans. You don't have to have a specific career goal in mind, but you should begin to do some long-range planning. These plans can help you formulate a direction for your undergraduate years. Begin a master plan of your course of study (adapted from Matthews, 1986). This master plan should extend through your entire college career. It should be flexible, because a course may not be offered during a particular semester, or two courses may meet at the same time, and so forth.

Consult your advisor when you draft your class schedule. Your advisor can help you to evaluate your reasons for choosing certain classes rather than others. When you meet with your advisor, have some idea of the classes you want to take for the coming semester. Consider alternatives and ask which would be best in terms of your master plan. By doing your scheduling this way, you can take full advantage of your advisor's insight and opinions as you develop your own ideas and direction. Remember, plan ahead!

Career counseling, however, may be an area for which your advisor is ill-prepared. Ask around to find out which advisors are knowledgeable about career planning. As you explore various careers for which you may be suited, visit your Career Placement Center for additional advice or career testing. You can then work together with both your faculty advisor and Career Placement Center advisor to plan an effective course of study. (Read chapter 7 on Career Placement Centers.)

If you have a particular interest in a profession already, talk to a faculty member or advisor in that particular department or field. He or she can advise you concerning suitable courses, minors, or graduate programs. That advisor might also have information on how to enter the field or profession upon graduation. Ask your own faculty advisor to recommend any special advisors or department staff who might be willing to meet with you.

Finally, remember that your faculty advisor will be a source of advice during your entire college career. There may be times when you need advice or direction that is not academic in nature, for which you need an impartial response. Most advisors are quite willing to help students find ways to deal with problems that are outside those areas they usually handle. If not, your advisor can refer you to help or guidance. In short, throughout your college career, look to your faculty advisor as a source of help in both academic and nonacademic matters.

References

Holloway, H. D. (1985). *Undergraduate psychology major program description.* Unpublished manuscript, North Texas State University, Department of Psychology, Undergraduate Committee.

Kulik, J. A. (1973). *Undergraduate education in psychology.* Washington, DC: American Psychological Association.

Matthews, J. R. (1986, August). What should students ask of their faculty advisors? In H. Takooshian (Chair), *Employment with a psychology BA.* Symposium conducted at the meeting of the American Psychological Association, Washington, DC.

How do psychology graduates feel about their degrees?

Will you be satisfied with a degree in psychology? Later in life, will you look back and wish you had sought another degree? The following information comes from a study of psychology majors who graduated from the University of Washington. Almost 800 people who had graduated over a 5-year period responded in a survey to the question, "If you had to do it over again, would you?" Nearly 70% of them said they would! Respondents to this survey also said that their degree was most satisfying in terms of their personal growth and liberal education. Of those who had also taken courses in business and computer science while undergraduates, satisfaction with their psychology degree was much greater.

Looking back at their college careers, these psychology graduates considered courses in statistics and courses with labs the least useful later on, especially for those who did not go on to graduate school. For those graduates, courses in child or personality development and social psychology were of greater value. Students who went to graduate school said research, fieldwork, and learning and physiological psychology courses were more beneficial.

Which skills and knowledge areas were most satisfying as a result of the psychology degree? Self-understanding, knowledge of people, and analytic thinking skills rated highest; writing and interpersonal skills rated lowest. Graduates pointed out that research, information gathering, and analytic thinking skills were most helpful for later employment and graduate preparation. Overall, psychology majors who went on to graduate school, including those who entered other graduate fields such as law, medicine, and dentistry, felt more satisfied with their major than those who did not.

Remember that you are more likely to value your degree in later years for contributing to your personal growth and providing you with a liberal arts education. This is true for almost any undergraduate degree program, unless it is one designed specifically to prepare you for graduate school or specific employment. You are likely to value your psychology major least in terms of career preparation, although your career possibilities will be wide ranging because of your degree. Skills that you can acquire through a psychology degree program, such as research, information gathering, and analytic thinking, can greatly improve your academic ability and enhance future job prospects. Self-understanding and knowledge of people can be tremendously important in whatever you decide to do. However, no undergraduate degree by itself, including psychology, can ever ensure employment. A degree can only make you more employable.

Degree options at the University of Washington

The University of Washington offers both a bachelor of science (BS) and a bachelor of arts (BA) degree in psychology. The BS is designed to prepare students for graduate study in psychology, and the bachelor of arts curriculum lets students prepare for immediate employment or other objectives. In contrast to the rigorous course requirements of the BS curriculum, only 50 quarter credits and a 2.0 grade point average are required of BA students. The only courses required are introductory psychology, methodology, statistics, and a lab course. The remaining 50 quarter credit hours are elective. Students studying for BAs are encouraged to supplement psychology with another field and to adopt a career orientation—in other words, to take both basic skills courses, such as English composition, and job-related skills courses, such as computer programming.

Maybe your school has a similar plan. Find out from the admissions office or psychology department whether such an option is offered. Then decide as quickly as you can which degree program you want to pursue. Do you want to enter graduate study or the business world after graduation? That choice is up to you.

PART 2

Psychology
and
career
preparation

Chapter 5

Building a bridge between two worlds: study and work

College can and should be the place for you to construct a personal bridge between the world of study and the world of work. For the most part, you have spent most of your life primarily in the world of study. While in the world of study, you have been encouraged to be dependent on the guidance of teachers in setting the course for your education. This was acceptable, because your teachers were primarily preparing you to move on to the next highest grade, and they knew better than you about how to prepare for continued advancement in the world of study. Now that you are in college, however, you will soon have to enter a world beyond that of study, the world of work.

If you are like most college students, first-hand knowledge of the world of work has come primarily from after-school and summer employment. Unfortunately, tasks like lawn mowing, burger frying, and grocery clerking involve activities largely unrelated to the type of occupation to which you aspire. The world of study is no more likely than part-time jobs to provide knowledge about the world of work. College, like all schools, is designed primarily to prepare you to advance to the next highest grade, not to prepare you for a career.

A bachelor's degree in the field of psychology, like an number of other fields, mainly prepares you for the next highest grade: graduate school. This is because most careers in psychology require the PhD degree. Positions requiring a bachelor's degree in psychology are rare. Nevertheless, undergraduate study in psychology can provide a valuable adjunct to study in other fields as preparation for your future career.

Moreover, although college is not designed to prepare you for employment, a majority of your college experiences can help you to solidify your career goals, develop marketable knowledge, skills, and abilities, and can even help you to develop contacts that can assist

Material for this chapter was contributed by Thomas F. Hilton, Naval School of Health Sciences, Bethesda, MD.

you in locating your first job. To do so, however, will require that you develop a strategy for building a bridge between the two worlds of study and work. This will include using college both to help establish career goals and to formulate an educational strategy to achieve those goals. Furthermore, your strategy must include developing *educational, social,* and *occupational* contacts that will enable you to cross your bridge when it comes time to enter the world of work.

Exercising fate control

College should be the place for you to construct a personal bridge between the world of study and the world of work. Preparing yourself for employment certainly should not be the only reason for going to college. However, a majority of your college experiences can form the basis of a career. An excellent way for you to ensure that graduation will mark the beginning of a challenging career is to exercise increased personal fate control throughout your educational process.

For most of your life you have been a student. Your education has been primarily in the hands of your teachers, counselors, and school administrators. They have decided which courses you were to take and what you were to learn, usually without considering your personal needs or preferences. Now, however, you are in college because you have chosen to be—and are probably paying a lot of money for the privilege. Now is the time to ensure that your purchase will be a sound investment. Now is the time to ensure that the product you receive, your education, will provide a bridge to the world of work.

Although it is possible to coast along for 4 years in college letting the "system" make most of your decisions for you, the system will not, and cannot, prepare you for the world of work. The system does, however, provide many

of the raw materials necessary to build a bridge to the world of work.

Setting career goals

Treating your college student role as a career is not merely a quaint metaphor. It signifies that you have consciously taken control of your own fate. It signifies that you have placed at the central focus of your life learning, learning about behavior, about yourself, about society, about the world of work. Treating college as a career is essential for constructing a bridge to the world of work. Treating college as a career is a serious path for success-oriented people.

The first step in treating your student role as a career is to establish career goals. Setting career goals is also important from a personal perspective. Most college students have an above average aptitude, and they are faced with what may seem to them to be limitless potential. Although long on career potential, most students are, unfortunately, short on actual work accomplishments on which to base career decisions. Consequently, narrowing can be a very frustrating task if you try to do it all at once. The central challenge of setting goals is trying to achieve a balance between what is personally desirable and what types of organizations or work settings you have access to.

Of course, career decision-making workshops are available on many campuses to help deal with the ambiguity of career decisions, and most schools have a career counseling staff that will be pleased to offer a variety of vocational preference inventories to help you organize your preferences. Although these activities are helpful for some students, they frequently turn out to be a disappointment because students tend to expect too much from them.

A good strategy is to use your classroom and life experiences in college to formulate and test hypotheses about yourself and establish career

goals accordingly. Your choice of psychology as a major will establish the general direction of the career goal-setting process. In addition, some narrowing of focus will occur as a result of what are called "career anchors," previous lifestyle choices such as marriage, children, geographic preference, and the college courses you have already taken. An hour or so of thoughtful reflection can help to derive a list of anchors that may help to narrow occupational choices somewhat.

Developing an education strategy

To help in setting career goals, consider and select appropriate *academic, social,* and *occupational* situations that will help you direct your education. One strategy is to construct a decision-making tree, which lists every course you think you would like to take until graduation. Each branch of your tree can represent a route to different types of jobs and work settings. Like the master plan you read about in chapter 4, the strategy behind decision-making trees is to help narrow your focus as you progress toward your goals. Narrowing is a process of elimination based on information developed at stages called decision points.

Assume that your college requires a core of courses in psychology that include at least one in both clinical and social psychology. If after taking abnormal psychology, you want to take other courses related to mental health, you could plan to take personality theory, then clinical psychology, group counseling, and later, a counseling practicum. After taking introductory social psychology, you could choose additional courses in that area, such as experimental social psychology, advanced social psychology, psychology of attitudes, group dynamics, and so forth.

If clinical psychology becomes less appealing to you over time, you could switch in emphasis to social psychology after finishing personality theory. Because that course, in this example, happens to be common to both areas, you should be able to change without starting over or taking additional courses. You can also do this if you plan to minor or take a concentration of supplementary career-oriented courses.

Remember, however, that course titles and areas of concentration for a psychology degree may vary from college to college. This hypothetical exercise may not reflect exactly the types of courses or requirements at your school. But the idea remains the same. After each semester or quarter, you should review and modify your tree based on what you have

learned about yourself. By using a decision-making tree, you can keep abreast of your standing, courses yet to take, options, and direction. You will control your education decisions. Such a strategy can help you efficiently manage your academic career and aid in setting your career goals.

Consider taking career-oriented courses outside the psychology department. There are a number of jobs with considerable career potential for which psychology training would be useful, especially when combined with knowledge from other fields. For example, a minor in business administration could provide an excellent background for work in the personnel department of many businesses. A minor in education could help certify you to teach psychology in high school or to work in special education. A minor in physical education could be useful in preparing for work in secondary education or with organizations such as the YMCA or YWCA.

Choosing social situations that can help in pursuit of your work career should also be a part of your education strategy. By participating in campus extracurricular activities, you can learn more about yourself and develop important social skills that may prove helpful in your future career. By joining a campus peer-counseling group, a suicide hotline, Big Brothers or Sisters, and so forth, you can gain valuable experience in counseling. By volunteering to work for almost any campus club or organization, you can gain experience in personnel organization or administration. Likewise, by joining a theater group, school band, or similar group, you can gain experience in both personnel administration and management. The point is, while in college, you can be exposed to possible career roles that can help you develop valuable interpersonal skills.

Exposure to work situations can be by far the most productive method for bridging the gap between the world of education and the world of work. Not only can you experience different work settings and tasks, but you can also learn how organizations actually function. Even small companies offer an opportunity to learn how various tasks are coordinated into the production of products and services.

Observe various workplaces and decide for yourself whether you prefer office settings, retail and service settings, or outdoor work, which usually involves moving from site to site. By working part-time or as an intern, you can show your skills and abilities to potential employers. This can lead to job referrals, references, and job offers.

Developing a network strategy

You no doubt have heard the phrase, "It's not what you know, but who you know." This statement does not mean that anyone can be successful as long as he or she has the right contacts. The statement underscores the importance of knowing how and where to tap into the network of connections that comprises the world of work in order to join that network. This complex network of connections are physical, geographic, economic, political, or interpersonal, and they must exist for commerce to carry on.

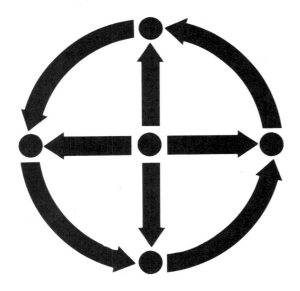

Finding your niche requires establishing contacts who can connect you and your special talents with those who might be interested in hiring you. This is important for two reasons. The likelihood of finding employment is a function of the degree to which you can convince an employer that you can make a unique contribution to the organization. Keep-

ing your job and being successful in it are both functions of the degree to which you can continue to make a unique and valuable contribution. The more your established contacts know about you, the better they will be able to connect you with the unique opportunity you're looking for, and the better you will be able to connect yourself to a job that's right for you.

A big mistake some college students make is to view the process of developing contacts as manipulative and deceitful instead of an enriching aspect of everyday life. This attitude may lead them to avoid seeking out people who have the capacity to play a critical role in helping them begin rewarding careers. Because we all live in a social world, we establish contacts with people nearly every day of our lives. Some of these contacts we nurture and develop in ways that enhance our quality of life. These contacts can become our friends, spouses, colleagues, employers, and so forth. By appreciating the importance of contacts in everyday life, we can help ourselves to identify potential occupational opportunities and exploit them to our advantage. You are not exploiting the individual contact who connected you with an opportunity. It is only the opportunity that you exploit—an opportunity for which you will have prepared yourself.

Part of the preparation process is excelling in your classroom studies. Don't believe it whenever you hear a student state that grades are unimportant and that employers never consider grades, just a diploma. The career-minded student knows that As and Bs are excellent evidence that he or she has actually acquired knowledge. High grades also serve as the primary way in which most employers judge whether you are capable of top achievement, and, both job and salary offers accordingly reflect this.

As your senior year rolls around, setting career goals should be fairly well in-hand, and you should be looking eagerly toward completing the final touches on your bridge to the world of work. At this point, it is a good idea to take inventory on the connections you have already established and to come to an understanding of how you can depend on your contacts to help find a job.

Academic contacts are helpful but sometimes limited. As you may remember from chapter 4, although your psychology advisor and professors can be helpful, their knowledge of the business world is usually limited to the education profession. They can offer guidance of a general nature, but are unlikely to possess specific knowledge about who is hiring psychology majors. However, those professors who have spent or spend the greatest amount of their time in the world of work, namely adjunct faculty, are most likely to serve as job connectors. Do not hesitate to talk to those faculty outside the psychology department and discuss ways to market your education and to identify job leads. Of course, faculty who are familiar with your career aspirations will be all the better suited to offer you assistance.

The extracurricular organizations you may elect to join are normally not very different from most work organizations. You can learn a great deal by observing how groups and social organizations coordinate functions and how you and other members react to the actions of leaders and others. Because few, if any, organizations are without problems, you can begin to learn how to identify problems and even solve them. You might possibly choose to try leadership roles to test your management and interpersonal skills. In addition to learning useful information applicable to work settings, extracurricular activities can also permit you to demonstrate achievement that can be brought to the attention of potential employers.

Some potential employers might include sponsors or nonstudent members of your group or social organization. In addition, many extracurricular activities involve interactions with individuals and organizations from the surrounding community. These activities can sometimes result in regular dealings with potential employers or those whose knowledge of you might help them to connect you with a job opportunity. Of course, you need to let people know that you are looking for an organization in which to build a career. Even if your graduation is a year or more off, some contacts can lead to part-time occupational situations that can help you reach your career goals.

Occupational contacts, of course, provide the best means of developing contacts who will lead to full-time employment. Some of the most helpful contacts for finding your first full-time position can be developed during part-time work, internships, or practica. Contacts developed in part-time work settings that most clearly resemble your career goals will be all the more suited to helping you find the right job. It is a good idea to find ways to work in at least one such setting during your college career.

Participation in your department's sponsored practica or internships are ways to establish occupational experience. Also, your college's Career Placement Center may be able to refer you to firms interested in part-time student employees. Even by approaching a company itself, you may be able to find career-related part-time work opportunities. In short, part-time work while in college is your most beneficial path to the world of work. It can help you enormously with deciding what career path to pursue as well as with your career later on.

Keep in mind that as a student employee you are likely to be viewed by many full-time co-workers as excess baggage. Because people in your work setting may be unprepared to utilize you effectively, you run a good chance of being assigned dull, routine, mundane tasks. Therefore, it is important not to get discouraged if this occurs and to show some hustle and creative initiative. (Read chapter 16 for insights.)

In conclusion, although some career goal-related positions may pay even less than burger frying, by the time graduation day comes around, your career orientation, your goal-setting, your judicious use of extracurricular experiences, your academic, social, and occupational contacts, and your part-time work investment can pay much higher dividends in terms of full-time earning power and finding a good job.

Exercising fate control after college

Remember that career building is a life-long process. As your career develops and your goals begin to move in new directions, you will begin to appreciate that the fate control process works just as well once you've entered the world of work. The career development literature shows that the majority of college graduates enter the world of work, and within a few years and a few promotions, settle into a job from which they are unlikely to move. Others continue the fate control process and continually grow in their careers. They continue to set career goals and to develop educational strategies to attain those goals.

What is important to graduate schools and to employers when considering applicants?

The question that eventually faces all undergraduates upon completing their bachelor's degree is whether to go to graduate school or to get a job. Although it may be a while before you make this decision, you should know what faculty and business people consider important when they look at applicants for admission or employment.

As part of a large national study (Milton, Pollio, & Eison, 1986), a questionnaire was sent to 500 faculty from 23 colleges and universities throughout the country and to 362 people in business and industry who were actively involved in interviewing and hiring college graduates. Both groups were asked to indicate the degree of importance they place on 15 items of information (e.g., standard test scores, grade point averages, jobs held, personality) when they consider students for either admission or employment. The results of the survey revealed that employers and faculty differ greatly in what they feel is important. For an undergraduate like yourself, the implications of such findings can be useful as you pursue your postgraduation opportunities. Table 6–1 is derived from the survey's findings and lists in order of importance those items employers and faculty look for when considering applicants.

As you can see, employers and graduate school administrators look for different traits and achievements in applicants. This difference reflects the needs and nature of both business and graduate school. Personality and individual presentation in the business world is fundamental; public speaking, interviewing others, and communicating are necessary skills for most employees, and job experience is a plus. Any student planning to go into business rather than graduate school should do some career-related or other part-time work while still in college.

Material for this chapter was contributed by John Edwards, Loyola University; James A. Eison, Southeast Missouri State University; and Kerry Smith, Loyola University. Edwards and Smith wish to thank Dr. Fred Bryant for his helpful comments and the following volunteer interviewers without whose assistance the Loyola University study would not have been completed: Don Allen, Sarah Brotherton, Susan Froula, Anne Herron, Pat Jorgenson, Kathy Kadlec, Joe Steffo, and expecially, Mary Pat Fowler and Jack Lamey.

Table 6-1

Business

1. Personality/presentation
2. Grades in major
3. Non-college jobs held

Graduate School

1. Number of difficult courses taken
2. Breadth of courses taken
3. Writing samples
4. Overall grade point average
5. Letters of recommendation
6. Publications, awards, honors

Note that although employers consider grades to be important, they consider those grades within your major to be more important. Graduate schools, on the other hand, take into account your overall grade point average. Keep in mind the emphasis that faculty place on academic and related activities. Business people emphasize performance and experience. These are important differences to remember as you choose which path to take.

What skills and knowledge do employers value most?

Most psychology majors initially do not go on to graduate school right after getting their bachelor's degree. Most of them enter the job market and often succeed in finding work that seems relevant to aspects of their undergraduate training. These jobs cover a wide range from mental health care worker in a hospital to research technician in government agencies or private organizations. To put it simply,

there are a multitude of employment opportunities awaiting you as a psychology major as long as you know where to find them and how to go about getting them.

As an undergraduate you need not restrict your future career direction to psychology-related endeavors simply because you are going to major in psychology. In the professional world, employers are not going to hire you for your degree, but for the skills and knowledge you acquire as you earn your degree. Some of the skills and knowledge areas employers look for when recruiting psychology majors are listed in this section. (For a detailed account of what you will encounter as an employee in the professional world, read chapter 16.)

As a psychology major, you have an opportunity to learn skills that are relevant to many types of careers, particularly those fields involving research. As you are taking courses, serving as an intern, or assisting in research or other activities, it is important to not only learn information, as part of your general education, but also to consider how the information translates into skills needed for research-related jobs. Psychology majors with appropriate course backgrounds and other experiences have proven that they can apply and extend their abilities to gather, analyze, and report information.

What, then, are the skills and knowledge areas employers look for when evaluating psychology majors as applicants? A recent survey of nearly 70 businesses and organizations in and around the Chicago area was conducted to help identify some of these skills and knowledge areas, particularly for positions that involve research. Managers and personnel representatives from a cross section of businesses were interviewed by telephone. (See box for more information on the survey.) The skills employers look for most, in order of importance, include abilities to

1. write proposals and reports
2. identify and solve problems based on research and knowledge of behavior
3. conduct interviews
4. do statistical analyses
5. design and conduct research projects

Knowledge areas include

1. attitude formation and change
2. personnel selection
3. individual thinking, information processing, and problem solving
4. structure and dynamics of small groups
5. effects of environment on people's feelings and actions

People in business are somewhat skeptical about the skills and knowledge that psychology majors are assumed to have. Business people prefer students with at least some business background who "speak the language." Of all the employers surveyed, most stressed internship experience as most valuable. Psychology majors with internship experience were considered more skillful, especially in areas such as statistical analysis, observing behavior, designing research, and writing proposals. Many employers said that administrative, analytical, and helping skills, as well as a knowledge of business practices and terminology are also of great value.

For this recent survey conducted at Loyola University of Chicago, researchers contacted employers in 69 businesses and agencies in and around the Chicago metropolitan area. These included nonprofit agencies engaged in advocacy or services, such as charitable or community organizations; federal, state, and local government agencies concerned with welfare, law enforcement, environmental quality, and education; retailers of appliances, clothing, food, and petroleum; and other for-profit corporations that sell services, such as banking, marketing, advertising, and management consulting. The nonprofit agencies preferred job applicants to have methodological skills (research design, conducting interviews, job analysis, and observation); government agencies and service corporations preferred data processing skills (coding, statistical analysis, and computer usage); and retailers preferred a mixture of skills (interviewing, job analysis, and computer usage).

Following is a list of the personal traits employers often look for when hiring. These are just as important to consider. Which do you believe you possess and which do you feel you lack? Keep in mind the traits you most need to develop and consciously work to acquire or improve them.

- the ability to work with others in a team
- motivation to work hard
- a positive attitude toward work
- leadership
- maturity
- flexibility
- the ability to communicate well
- intelligence
- the ability to solve problems
- integrity
- tolerance for stress
- honesty
- organizational ability

Some skills and knowledge areas seem more highly regarded by employers than others. The ability to write, to apply knowledge in solving problems, and to employ certain skills such as interviewing and statistical analysis are more favorable than other skills, such as observing behavior or administering tests. In general, employers regard knowledge in the social or organizational areas of psychology more highly than other areas, such as personality, developmental, or abnormal psychology. This may well be something to keep in mind throughout your college career.

Also, keep in mind that there are always exceptions to what employers want or see in any potential employee. The relative importance of various skills, knowledge, and personal traits will vary from one employer to another. Hiring new employees is at times a subjective and personal process. Knowing where to find employment opportunities and how to go about getting them is only half the journey. Remember to follow your interests and capabilities, not only for employment but through life, and opportunities will be sure to come your way!

References

Milton, O., Pollio, H., & Eison, J. (1986). *Making sense of college grades: Why the grading system does not work and what can be done about it.* San Francisco, CA: Jossey-Bass.

Pilla, L. (1984, October). The job search: What college students say. *Management World, p. 19.*

Characteristics Employers Look For in Entry-Level Job Candidates

In a recent survey (Pilla, 1984) the American Management Society asked its member employers to select from 9 traits the most important characteristic the employers seek in candidates applying for entry-level positions. The percent of respondents rating each item as most significant is as follows:

enthusiasm/motivation	35%
education background	20%
communication skill	16%
scholastic performance	12%
intelligence	5%
work-related experience	2%
interpersonal/leadership skill	2%
maturity	2%
creativity	0%

Chapter 7

At your service: the career placement center

Like many college students, you probably have at the present time only a rudimentary understanding of the professional world. This is quite understandable. Your primary contacts have been and will continue to be with faculty and fellow students. The world of education is all around you, and the pursuit of your degree probably consumes most of your time and energy. Questions about future career plans tend to have less importance to you now than does the fulfillment of your academic interests and requirements.

However, as you recall from chapter 5, developing an educational strategy is vital for career goal setting while still in college and for your future success. You would not want to find yourself in your senior year without a plan, objectives, or a focus for the future. Sometime in your college career, you may decide that graduate school, for instance, is not an option. If so, what are you to do? How do you begin directing yourself toward a successful future?

Fortunately, there is, in virtually every college and university today, a major source of assistance called the Career Placement Center (or a similar name). Its staff are responsible for assisting students, regardless of major, to determine their professional direction through counseling and self-assessment and to enhance their career awareness and alternatives. Career Placement Centers exist to assist students in clarifying their career goals. Although the lack of career goals may not prevent you from finding work after you graduate, the fact is that a first job may not lead you to the career you want. What, then, is involved in making a career choice? What will the staff at the center suggest when you approach them with your unfocused future in your backpack?

Career Placement Center staff prefer to make their first contact with students considerably earlier than the last 2 weeks of school—in fact, earlier than your senior year. There are

Material for this chapter was contributed by Bernardo J. Carducci, Indiana University Southeast, and Marilyn S. Walters, University of Southern Indiana. The contributors would like to express their appreciation to James A. Kanning, Donna Klein, and Jan Hamblen for their assistance in the gathering of information for this chapter.

many tasks that you can be doing to ensure that you are well prepared upon graduation to address the job market. For example, many centers offer courses or workshops in job-search strategies. These tend to focus on resume writing and job interviewing (see chapters 13 and 14.) Although these workshops are important, the strategies that really count are those you should start employing as a sophomore or junior.

If you follow the guidelines presented in this chapter, any anxiety you may feel about your future should be reduced. The effort and preparation that you invest in the early stages will lay the foundation for success in the future. By using the resources of your Career Placement Center, you will not only develop career goals and direction but also gain a better understanding of the world of work as well.

Ideally, Career Placement Centers should provide students with the assistance and resources they need to find jobs and make proper career choices. However, not all such centers operate in the same way. Your university may utilize a computer-assistance guidance program or rely on personal counseling, supplemented by printed and audio-visual materials. Ultimately, it is up to you to take full advantage of the resources available there.

What do you like?
Assessing your interests

Career Placement Centers have several valuable resources, but none are more valuable than the placement counselors. As you become familiar with the center, get to know the counselors and maintain frequent contact throughout your college career. If possible, make a formal appointment with one to get acquainted. Be as frank and as open as you can. Placement counselors are there for you, to help you focus your career goals. Don't feel intimidated; respond openly and ask questions.

The placement counselor will probably ask you about your interests. What do you like to do, and what would you like to get paid to do, given the chance? Your counselor might ask you to take an interest inventory. This will help you define your likes and dislikes and see how they relate to a variety of occupational possibilities, school subjects, general and leisure activities, and types of people. After taking the inventory, your interest patterns can then be compared with those of individuals working in a variety of fields.

Your counselor can help you see what occupations closely match your interest patterns. For example, if your interests show that you like (a) being in social interactions, such as being with and showing concern for the welfare of others; (b) being enterprising, such as leading others; and (c) being conventional, such as preferring ordered activities, then your counselor might show you some possible career alternatives (librarian, fundraiser, disk jockey, federal aid coordinator, or production manager).

Don't be misled, however, into believing that the results of interest inventories are quick and simple answers to your career questions. These career alternatives are not necessarily what you should do. They merely allow you to compare your pattern of interests with those of people in various existing occupations. They give you suggestions for potential career choices. While these interest inventories will not tell you what to do, they are a very good source of expanding your awareness of careers you might enjoy.

What can you do?
Assessing your abilities

Although everyone hopes to find work doing what he or she enjoys, your interests alone are not enough upon which to make a career choice. Your counselor might recommend certain follow-up activities, such as assessing your skills.

- Do you have good communication skills?
- How effective are you at organizing and synthesizing data?
- Do you interact well with people?
- Are you an effective motivator, counselor, manager, or teacher?

Ask yourself about your own special skills. Remember to consider the skills you have developed specifically as a result of pursuing a degree in psychology.

It is as important to know what you need to improve as it is to know where your strengths lie. Your placement counselor might be able to help you identify your special talents and also help you assess how best to develop other important skills. For example, if you fear public speaking, your first instinct might be to avoid public speaking classes altogether. In actuality, your reluctance to speak before groups will eventually limit your career advancement. Career counselors can help you determine ways to overcome weak areas in your occupational skills.

What do you want at work? Assessing your work values

Finally, your counselor should encourage you to consider your work values.

- What do you hope to receive from your work aside from an adequate salary?
- Do you prefer work that's highly structured and supervised or work requiring greater initiative and self-organization?
- What level of status, mobility, security, and personal interaction do you desire?
- Would you want a demanding, high-power position or an 8-to-5 job that allows more leisure time?
- What kind of life-style do you want by ages 30, 40, and 50? What are you willing to do to get there?

Only when you can articulate the interests, abilities, and work values you possess will you be ready to examine the huge variety of occupational choices available to you.

Doing research on occupations

Among the most important resources available at most Career Placement Centers are the occupational materials that permit you to explore various career options. You may want to read further about some of the career fields that you identified through your interest inventory. Additionally, the Placement Center staff can help you learn to use a number of the major career-reference textbooks and periodicals, containing information on thousands of occupations. These reference materials provide even more alternatives appropriate for someone with your unique combination of em-

ployment needs. The *Dictionary of Occupational Titles* (U.S. Department of Labor, 1977) contains information portraying the characteristics of most jobs in the American economy. The *Occupational Outlook Handbook* (U.S. Department of Labor, 1984) describes the nature of work, places of employment, qualifications, advancement, employment outlook, earnings, working conditions, and other sources of information on more than 800 occupations.

Making contact

After examining these occupational materials and talking to your placement counselor, you will have compiled a manageable list of career possibilities. Now would be the time to schedule some informational interviews with professionals in the community.

An informational interview differs from a job interview in that you are doing the interviewing. You are seeking information from an employer about the profession, the skills and knowledge he or she seeks when hiring employees, and general perceptions of work and employees. For a further explanation of the informational interview, see chapter 14. To help you with arranging informational interviews, many Career Placement Centers keep lists of employers, many of them alumni, who have volunteered to talk to students. Your placement counselor can help you formulate questions to ask in the interview as well as brief you on proper etiquette.

Getting experience

As suggested earlier, to give yourself an additional edge, consider participating in cooperative education or internship programs. These types of programs allow you to gain experience in your desired field while you make more professional contacts. They also give you the opportunity to work in a particular position. It could be that after doing a particular job, you decide that it is not what you thought it would be.

The cooperative education or internship administrator may be located in the Career Placement Center or in another department. Your own psychology department may provide this service. Be prepared to explain exactly the work experience and work environment you are seeking.

Register early

Be sure that you are properly registered with the Career Placement Center early on. Your defined job objective will allow the staff to assist you more effectively. Job leads do not appear only in the 2 weeks prior to graduation. Early registration will allow you to receive notification of every opening that is consistent with your stated career goals.

Continue to cultivate your network of contacts. Let faculty, family, and friends know exactly what type of position you are seeking. What if the ideal job became available 4 months before graduation? Learn to go beyond the classified ads. Over 75% of job vacancies available on any given day are not advertised. Your Career Placement Center can help you tap into the real job market through its various resources.

The tools for an effective job search

The Career Placement Center can also help you put together the tools for your job search. Career Placement Centers usually offer classes or clinics on writing résumés. You should learn the appropriate style and format of résumés and how to construct a cover letter. (For an explanation of the résumé and the cover letter, see chapters 13 and 14.) Once you have completed a draft of your résumé, your placement counselor can help you improve it. Together, the two of you can tackle the various aspects of grammar, organization, style, and substance to refine your résumé. It is at this point that your contact with the Career Placement Center can pay off. Your counselor must know enough about you to help you effectively and guide you in the right direction.

You should also take job-search workshops offered by the center. A job-search workshop should include tips not only on surviving the job interview, but on actually blossoming under this intense scrutiny. Your placement counselor can provide you with a list of questions most frequently asked during interviews. This allows you to prepare effective answers. Some counselors also videotape role-playing interviews. You and a counselor can then critique your interviewing style, giving you the opportunity to eliminate any distracting mannerisms and revise any ineffective responses.

In the end, it is still up to you

Although a relatively small percentage of undergraduates actually secure their first jobs through on-campus recruiting by employers, your Career Placement Center can provide a highly visable service. Sign up for interviews, and test the waters! With the practical knowledge you have gained through your visits and work with the center, this is the next logical step for you to take.

The common job-search characteristics that successful job applicants share are a positive self-image, clearly articulated career goals, and the ability to sell their skills, work backgrounds, and desirable traits to an employer. The psychology major reaches this point by the same process as does the marketing major, the English major, or the biology major. The Career Placement Center is one of the most important resources on campus for those students who look to the future, desiring to guide their job search, rather than be manipulated by the market. The best advice for you is to visit the Career Placement Center early in your academic career, and visit it often thereafter. If you have not done so yet, do so now. Although job-search assistance is available, it's still up to you whether, and how well, you take advantage of it.

References

U.S. Department of Labor. (1977). *Dictionary of occupational titles* (4th ed.). Washington, DC: U.S. Government Printing Office.

U.S. Department of Labor. (1984). *Occupational outlook handbook* (1984-1985 ed.). Washington, DC: U.S. Government Printing Office.

PART 3

Psychology majors in the workplace: traditional and unconventional careers

Chapter 8

Are you interested in a business career?

An entry-level position in business is one very promising career path available to many psychology majors. However, to compete successfully with business majors and other students for these positions, the psychology major must possess certain basic business skills and knowledge. To help prepare you as a psychology major for a career in business, this chapter will cover (a) the basic skills you will need to be successful in business, (b) some of the basic decisions you will need to make when seeking a business career path, (c) a curriculum strategy you might wish to use as a guideline to help prepare you for a business career, and (d) how and why you should become more involved in the business community.

Basic business skills

To compete successfully with business majors in areas such as management, personnel, marketing, and sales, you must possess and be able to demonstrate specific personal attributes necessary to step into entry-level business positions. Employers consider the following four attributes to be vital for individuals in entry-level positions:

1. An understanding of goal-directed behavior. This includes an understanding that sometimes goals are set by forces beyond an individual's control.
2. An understanding of the nature and process of solving problems. This includes how to recognize problems, analyze situations, develop alternatives, and make decisions.
3. The ability to communicate with others. This includes abilities to write clearly, speak clearly, and listen effectively.

Material for this chapter was contributed by Bernardo J. Carducci, Indiana University Southeast.

4. An understanding of human behavior, including the ability to become a leader and motivate others.

The variety of skills associated with these four basic attributes can be grouped into three categories: technical skills, conceptual skills, and human skills. Technical skills are those needed to perform the task at hand. If you want to become an accountant or marketing analyst, you need to possess some skills related to fundamental accounting or basic marketing practices. You can acquire these skills in business courses. If you want to be a personnel manager, the technical skills needed range from interviewing techniques to testing methods. These skills can be acquired in counseling and clinical psychology courses.

Conceptual skills have to do with an understanding of "the big picture." In business, you must have an understanding of where your job fits within the organization and how it relates to other job functions. Without this understanding, you will operate in a vacuum and become easily disenchanted with your career objective. Conceptual skills can be developed in a variety of advanced courses in psychology involving the integration of many different theoretical viewpoints. Human skills are those skills that enable you to understand human behavior and communication. These skills can be acquired in courses such as sociology, psychology, speech and theater, and creative writing.

Given these basic attributes, it should be very clear that many of the skills and much of the knowledge necessary for you to compete successfully for entry-level positions in business can be acquired in disciplines other than the business department, most notably in psychology. The major function of the business

portion of your curriculum is to teach you how conceptual and human skills can be utilized in the business workplace. To best prepare yourself for a career in business, make an effort to take nonpsychology courses that will help you to develop these basic business skills.

Deciding which business courses to take

In addition to acquiring these basic business skills, you will need to decide on the type of business career you want to pursue. The business courses you take will provide the necessary technical skills and help in this decision making. Such courses include principles of economics (3-6 credit hours), introduction to business administration (3 credit hours), and introduction to accounting (6 credit hours).

After taking these courses, you should know enough to at least begin narrowing your career choices. In addition, by developing some answers to the following questions you might gain a greater sense of your career direction. Answer those questions you are most sure of and gather information to help answer the rest.

- What particular industry am I most interested in: banking, retailing, or "high-tech" companies?
- What size firm would I like to work for: Fortune 500, a medium-sized firm, or a small local firm?
- What area or function in business interests me most: marketing, sales, training, research and development, management, or personnel?
- What is my ultimate career objective: vice-president, upper-level manager, director, or staff supervisor?
- Which of the following would I most, and least, like to depend on in my career: technical skills (production management, systems analysis), conceptual skills (marketing or strategic planning), or human skills (personnel or training)?

A curriculum strategy

The curriculum strategy proposed here is, for the most part, a business minor for arts and science majors. The business minor, depending on your school's requirements, should consist of 24 to 27 credit hours and include introduction to accounting, principles of economics, and introduction to business administration. The accounting course is taught in most colleges as a two-course sequence. You should complete the sequence by the second semester of your sophomore year. Principles of economics can be taken in either the freshman or sophomore year. The introduction to business administration course should be taken in the freshman year or as soon as possible, because it provides a framework for many of the career decisions you will be making later. These courses will compose the core 12-15 hours of the proposed minor.

Additional business coursework will depend on your specific career interests. For example, if you are interested in a career in marketing, supplement the core courses with introduction to marketing (3 credit hours), marketing research (3 credit hours), and a choice of advertising, marketing strategy, or consumer behavior (3 credits each).

Some nonbusiness courses that are highly recommended include an introductory course in computer programming and courses in statistics, interpersonal communications, public speaking, social stratification, and demography. Finally, specific psychology courses that are highly recommended for psychology majors considering careers in business include social psychology, psychology of personality, human motivation, psychology of learning, industrial/organizational psychology, perception, experimental/research methods, and cognitive psychology.

Become involved in the business community

To maximize your success when pursuing a career in business, you must become involved with the local business community. Get to know faculty members in the business department as well as in the psychology department. Becoming familiar with both departments can benefit you greatly because both disciplines can provide you with educational experiences not available separately from either department.

You should also use the services of the Career Placement Center on your campus. As you read in chapter 7, the Career Placement Center offers many services (career counseling, interviewing skills, resume preparation, and so forth) and educational opportunities (internships and cooperative education programs with local business firms). Such opportunities are not typically provided by psychology departments, but internship and similar experiences are extremely helpful when you seek employment in business. You should also visit local business firms to discuss what they view as important when they consider psychology majors for entry-level positions. A list of cooperative employers can probably be obtained from the Career Placement Center.

You have undoubtedly heard someone say, "I really enjoy psychology, but I am going to major in something that qualifies me for a job after I graduate, like business." Many students have the misconception that there is a lack of employment opportunities for psychology majors. And as a result of the tightening job market, many potential psychology majors are electing to pursue degrees in other disciplines that appear to provide better job prospects. This loss of psychology graduates can be reversed by providing you and other psychology majors with the skills and knowledge necessary to compete successfully for entry-level positions in a variety of business fields.

There are, in fact, many things you can do with your psychology degree. However, you have to decide if you want to become a psychologist, which will require at least 5 to 9 additional years of graduate education, or if you want to use your knowledge of psychology in the business world as an assistant personnel manager, a training and staff development supervisor, or a marketing research account officer. Many psychology majors have traditionally overlooked this alternative in business when asking that all-too-familiar question, "What can I do with my psychology degree?"

Chapter 9

Human factors careers in high tech

Are you interested in modern technology, in what its processes and products do to human behavior—or in what people do to technology? A dynamic and engaging branch of psychology brings psychology and technology together. It goes by many names — human factors psychology, engineering psychology, human factors, ergonomics. Psychologists in this field investigate human and technology interactions and apply what is known about these.

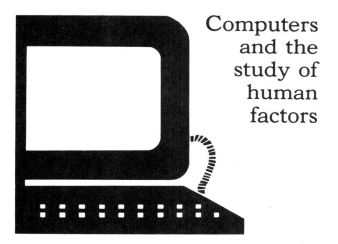

Computers and the study of human factors

The use of personal computers in the workplace has stimulated interest in human factors psychology in recent years. IBM, AT&T, GTE, and other companies have expanded their human factors groups, hiring psychologists and programmers to study the interactions between computers and users, the performance of programmers, and the design of data bases and software interfaces. Chances are that sometime in your future you will either study or find employment in situations involving modern technology. You may come to realize that research may be even inspired by technology's human-related problems.

Material for this chapter was contributed by H. McIlvaine Parsons, Essex Corporation, Alexandria, VA.

Within the American Psychological Association, human factors psychology members compose Division 21, Applied Experimental and Engineering Psychologists. Most of them are also members of the Human Factors Society, a multidisciplinary organization with about 4,000 members, a journal, annual meetings, 12 local chapters, and 5 student chapters.

The International Ergonomics Association is composed of societies in the United States, England, Japan, West Germany, Scandinavia, France, Holland, Poland, Czechoslovakia, and other countries, making the growth of the field worldwide.

Human factors psychologists have also continued to pursue interests in hardware-oriented technologies such as the following:

- aircraft and spacecraft
- radar and sonar
- highway and urban transportation
- telephone and radio communications
- office and postal operations
- mining and nuclear power plants
- air traffic control
- military command and control systems
- manufacturing

As modern technology has become more complex and information-based, so has human factors psychology. Human factors psychologists mainly study human performance in the workplace and "in-the-head" operations involving attention, memory, decision making, and problem solving. They also study accuracy and productivity to reveal human capabilities and limitations.

From the knowledge they gain, human factors psychologists can participate in the design of equipment, work environments, or computer programs, formulate procedures, or test the designs work. They may study what makes computers "unfriendly" in either software or hardware design. They may measure job satisfaction and, indeed, increase it by changing the features of the job. Alternatively, they may develop training or selection techniques to adapt an operator to a design—activities sometimes under the label "human resources."

Users of modern technology function in business, academia, government, and industry. Social interactions in these areas are influenced by technology. If you are interested in modern technology and how it applies to human behavior, you should be aware it is used in organizational settings.

Preparing for a career in human factors psychology

As an undergraduate major in psychology, how can you prepare for a career as a human factors psychologist? Unless you have substantial training in data processing or engineering, graduate school is essential, whether you want to work in industry, business, consulting, government, or academia. Employment in applications work as a human factors psychologist usually requires at least a master's degree, with additional graduate study or work experience if you wish to engage in research.

Therefore, as an aspiring undergraduate you need to know (a) what to study as an undergraduate and (b) where to get graduate training in order to work as a human factors psychologist. It is important to lay a foundation of skills now, in conjunction with a psychology degree. Here are some initial suggestions.

- Learn to write and speak lucidly and succinctly.

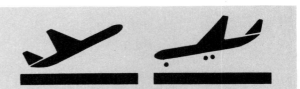

One of the earliest challenges faced by human factors psychologists, almost 40 years ago, was designing an aircraft altimeter. How should it be designed so that the pilot would not misread it and fly the plane into the ground—as had often happened? More recently, after the nuclear accident at Three Mile Island, human factors psychologists were asked how the many control room panels in nuclear power plants could be designed to eliminate operator error. Human factors psychologists have also been studying "mental workload." Does the quality of work performance degrade when workload is too heavy, and what does this workload consist of? Can laboratory methods for measuring mental workload be applied in the field? Such challenges enliven this branch of psychology, and scientists working in universities, industry, and government have risen to them.

- Acquire some knowledge of calculus and statistics.
- Become competent in one or two computer programming languages.
- Learn research methods such as experimental design and survey.
- Take a course in human physiology or physiological psychology.
- Emphasize the study of the senses and perception, learning, perceptual motor skills, and thinking processes.
- Acquire some familiarity with electronics and mechanics.
- Study language semantics and structure.

With respect to graduate study, you face a more complex problem. Educational requirements differ, of course, between the master's and doctoral levels, and from institution to institution. If, however, your aspirations point you in the direction of equipment and system design applications, also called human factors engineering, you should take engineering or computer science courses, if possible in a human factors engineering program, in addition to advanced psychology and methodology courses. If you move in the direction of becoming a practitioner in training or some related field, such as job performance aids, you may want to place more emphasis on courses in human learning, thinking, and motivation, as well as computer programming.

With which experts does the human factors psychologist associate? These may be industrial, electrical and electronic, or mechanical engineers as well as aeronautical, civil, automotive, and manufacturing engineers. Human factors in computers, or "software psychology," is taught in departments of computer science, and the human factors psychologist can expect to work with programmers, analysts, and computer scientists in studying user performance, programming, and artificial intelligence. Some human factors psychologists have become involved in environmental design, which allows them to work with architects, interior designers, office designers, naval architects, acousticians, or lumination engineers. Those interested in consumer products may work with industrial designers. Those concerned with the techniques of training may work with training specialists and educational psychologists. And those concerned with organizational and personnel matters may benefit from contact with industrial/organizational psychologists. Clearly, anyone becoming a human factors psychologist should expect to work with other disciplines, especially in applications.

Chapter 10

What about a career in law?

The link between psychology and law

L aw school? Prelaw? Do these disciplines sound alien to you as a psychology major? What does psychology have in common with law? How can a degree in psychology prepare you for law school and a career in law? You may be surprised to learn that the link between psychology and law is more obvious than you think. And as preparation for not only law school but for law practice, a psychology degree can be a valuable tool and resource.

According to a recent university survey, psychology graduates who eventually enter law school typically wait several years after college before they apply. Usually these graduates initially take entry-level jobs in either a human services or a government agency. Probation officers, welfare caseworkers, caretakers, and psychiatric aides often deal with personal concerns of their clients that are directly related to the clients' legal problems. These problems can include child and spouse abuse, trouble with the police, complex financial arrangements, welfare payments, drug addiction, and so forth. Further, the link between psychology and the practice of law is always present in the working lives of professional psychologists, aides, and caseworkers, if only because laws govern how, where, and when they can practice.

To study law is to study human behavior. A psychology background can give you an empirical perspective on the law and add insight into legal theories and decisions that cannot be obtained solely through the study of law. Additionally, psychology majors tend to possess a special insight in areas of mental health law, criminal law, and family law, where relevant evidence is often based in psychology. Without a knowledge of psychology, critical un-

Material for this chapter was contributed by Elizabeth V. Swenson, John Carroll University.

derstanding of specific legal arguments in these areas may be superficial.

The late legal scholar Karl N. Llewellyn listed the following skills that he thought a student should acquire through prelegal education:

- reading and writing well
- using a library
- evaluating opinion and evidence both qualitatively and quantitatively
- assessing people (Vanderbilt, 1981, p. 31)

Ideally, reading, writing, using a library, and qualitative evaluation are skills nurtured through a general liberal arts education. However, an undergraduate psychology curriculum focuses specifically on quantitative evaluation and assessing people. In addition, psychology majors learn to analyze factual situations in a logical and concise manner, which is essential for legal studies.

A psychology degree can prepare you for law school in the same ways it can prepare you for legal practice later on. The lawyer's job has been described as one that deals with the interaction of rules of law, facts, and people (Vanderbilt, 1981, p. 18). This is similar to the study of theory, empirical results, and individual differences by the psychologist. Counseling is another skill essential for practicing law. To put yourself in another person's shoes is important for interviewing clients and witnesses and for negotiating and arbitrating.

Preparing for a career in law

How should psychology majors who are considering a career in law prepare themselves as undergraduates? First, take several experimental psychology and statistics courses and obtain as much research and writing experience as possible. A course in counseling is very useful, as well as one in social psychology in order to grasp aspects of jury dynamics, eyewitness testimony, and plea bargaining. Also, courses that offer knowledge of abnormal behavior, psychological tests, and mental

health institutions are important in understanding substantive legal issues.

The American Bar Association (1980) recommends that prelegal studies educate students for comprehension and expression in words, critical understanding of human institutions and values, and creative power in thinking. In conjunction with these suggestions, the following subject areas are recommended to supplement your psychology degree:

- writing and public speaking
- argumentation and debate, which will help you to frame arguments, back them up with evidence, and think under pressure
- Western political thought and the history of Western civilization
- philosophy courses in logic and ethics, which are fundamental to legal thought
- introductory physics and biology, which will help you to remain in touch with developments in science and technology
- American politics and international relations
- introduction to economics
- basic accounting, to understand aspects of business law
- any computer language course, to help with computerized legal research

Many undergraduate programs offer separate law courses, such as criminal law, constitutional law, family law, or business law. Although it is generally unwise to take these courses, which will be repeated in law school, one such law course might be beneficial on the undergraduate level for you to get a feel for the format of legal opinions or to help you decide whether the study of law may be of interest later on.

References

American Bar Association. (1980). *Law schools and professional education.* Chicago: Author.
Vanderbilt, A. T., III. (1981). *Law school: Briefing for a legal education.* New York: Penguin Books.

Chapter 11

Emerging and unconventional careers for psychology majors

Why should the task of informing students like yourself about careers be so difficult, especially in a nation whose prosperity depends on the successful match between jobs and those who have the talent for them? At least part of the reason lies in the nature of our technological society. Technological change is occurring so rapidly that literally hundreds of careers become obsolete while hundreds of new careers are created. Such rapid changes have led futurists to predict that as many as 80% of the jobs that will exist by the end of the century are not even in existence today!

This chapter highlights some emerging and unconventional careers that would provide interesting opportunities for you as a psychology major who is planning a nonacademic career. Frequently, such emerging careers do not have easily identifiable titles, partly because many have yet to become fully established. Many of these careers do not require specialized graduate training.

Health psychology

Behavioral medicine and behavioral health. Nowhere are the boundaries between traditional disciplines dissolving more quickly than in the field of behavioral medicine. Behavioral medicine is multidisciplinary and includes psychiatry, medicine, clinical psychology, social psychology, health education, communication, biostatistics, clinical epidemiology, and journalism (Bazar, 1980). Behavioral medicine recognizes the role of behavior in the development of health problems and the expertise of psychologists to change such behavior. Programs may focus on prevention or treatment.

For example, the Stanford Heart Disease Prevention Program explores techniques of modifying life-styles that are thought to contribute to heart disease. Such "wellness" programs

Material for this chapter was contributed by Michael J. Zeller, Mankato State University, with material reprinted from Careers in Psychology.

make people aware that the way they live is making them healthy or ill (McCrary, 1983). Another prevention effort focuses on reducing the number of babies born with physical or mental defects, which has doubled over the last 25 years. Educating pregnant women to possible risks and intervening to modify those behavioral patterns that contribute to these problems is an important contribution that psychologists trained in a multidisciplinary perspective could make. Businesses are realizing that changing life-styles can play an important role in keeping employees healthy and lowering hospital and insurance costs. Treatment programs help clients quit smoking, reduce weight, control diabetes and hypertension, modify compulsive work habits, control chronic pain, reduce stress on lower backs, overcome chronic anorexia or bulimia, and control the symptoms of psychosomatic disorders.

Biofeedback therapy. Biofeedback is gaining acceptance as a means of increasing awareness of responses to stress and teaching voluntary control over physiological responses. The Biofeedback Institute of San Francisco reports that biofeedback has proved acceptable and marketable to the general public. The ads promote the use of biofeedback to cure or control migraines, insomnia, epilepsy, asthma, stuttering, and sexual disorders. The Institute has pioneered a stress management program by opening offices in San Francisco's financial district.

Therapists trained at the Institute are typically physicians, psychologists, or social workers. The Biofeedback Institute currently trains 100 practitioners a year. The Biofeedback Society of America already has over 1,500 members and societies in 12 states (Freeman, 1980).

Treating phobias. The medical and psychological professions have identified a group of people who experience panic attacks in public places for no apparent reason. They suffer from what is called agoraphobia. Misdiagnosed in the past, these people often developed life-crippling fears, became recluses, and in some cases, believed they were going crazy or having heart attacks.

At least six programs for treating agoraphobia now exist. The treatment program at Abbott-Northwestern Hospital in Minneapolis is based on the theory that these people fear loss of control. Their treatment involves learning about the nervous system and reactions to stress, general skills for coping with anxiety, and how to use these skills in the situations in which they are experiencing their attacks. An estimated 2.5 million Americans could ben-

efit from such treatment (Watson, 1983). Treatment procedures have also been developed to treat other debilitating phobias, including those of mathematics and computers.

Promoting human welfare using pets and trained animals. The human-animal bond is used to promote human welfare. Studies suggest that pets help older people maintain good physical and mental health (Schellhardt, 1983). Carefully selected and trained animals are being used to facilitate the recovery of the chronically mentally ill, treat patients with hypertension, increase the involvement and activity of handicapped children, and serve as eyes for the blind and ears for the deaf. Monkeys have even been trained to aid the physically handicapped.

Profiling for prediction. Profiling, the description of individual personalities, and the use of the profiles to understand motives and to predict behavior, has widespread application. Profiling can also be used to predict which persons are prone to heart attacks or heart disease by means of examining risk factors found to have correlations with heart attacks and heart disease. Some companies are developing such profiles for their executives in the belief that intervention in high-risk cases can prevent the death or disability of a valuable staff member.

Applications of technology for producing genes in the laboratory is on the verge of making it possible to predict disease in individuals years before it occurs (Bishop, 1983). Genes made in the laboratory are used to sift through one's genetic material and identify genes that may predispose people to cancer, heart disease, and other illnesses.

Psychology and children

Counseling children in medical and dental settings. A new speciality is developing that might be called pediatric psychology. Psychological techniques can reduce the fear and stress that children often suffer in medical and dental settings. For example, the Children's Hospital in Philadelphia scents gas masks for anesthesia with the smell of root beer or licorice. Puppets have been used to provide education regarding medical procedures and to prevent surprises ("Doctors Treat," 1977). Some psychologists are specialists in developing ways of teaching children what pain is and how to cope with it. Psychologists are also concerned with children being treated for cancer and other chronic diseases.

Caring for children of working parents. The sharp rise in the number of working mothers, especially among those with small children, has created an unprecedented demand for day-care and related child-care services. There are an estimated 6.5 million latchkey children, children who must spend at least part of the day at home alone because their parents work outside the home (Hunt, 1984).

The response to this problem has been slow and limited, but it is gradually increasing. Every community has a variety of child-care programs and often a referral center to match the needs of parents with available services. Employers are realizing that the availability of child care has an impact on employee morale, productivity, and turnover. More than 450 U.S. companies now provide on-site day-care, and 1,000 companies offer some kind of child-care support. Of 15,000 school districts, 125 now provide for some after-hours activities. There are "Phonefriend" or "Warmline" services that provide latchkey children an adult to talk with in over 200 cities (Lublin, 1984). As legislative support for programs at state and national levels is mobilized and more employees demand services from employers as part of fringe benefits, the need to staff day-care, latchkey programs, and referral services can be expected to grow dramatically.

Discovering and nurturing giftedness. Gifted students have been historically neglected because educators felt that the gifted neither needed nor deserved any special help or attention to achieve their potential. However, interest in gifted education may be about to surge (Cunningham, 1984). In conjunction with this interest, discovery of gifted individuals becomes a primary challenge. Nurturing the gifted presents an additional challenge. This includes making gifted students and their families aware of special educational opportunities, as well as counseling parents who often are the first to suspect that their child is gifted.

Many other roles exist for those who would help the gifted. For instance, many gifted students often have unmet emotional needs simply because they are different. Also, other emerging needs could include developing programs that challenge the gifted (50% of them are underachievers), providing awareness programs for teachers, and developing resource rooms.

Developing metacognition. A number of psychologists and educators are working on metacognition, a child's understanding of his or her own thinking and reasoning skills. They suggest that as children become more competent in skills, their awareness of mental strategies emerges, and they are able to use the strategies more independently and spontane-

ously. Ways to teach these cognitive skills include direct instruction in reading, participatory learning, mediated learning, the Socratic method, and reciprocal teaching in which students teach other students or teachers (Cordes, 1984).

Promoting animal welfare. People from a wide variety of backgrounds can contribute their skills as teachers for animal welfare programs. The Society for the Prevention of Cruelty to Animals has designed a 4-month program for grade schoolers. The goals of the program are to get youngsters thinking about the relationships between animals and humans. Topics include animal-related careers, humane issues, and pet care and responsibility (Gaiter, 1984).

Another area of growing demand is for outdoor nature education for children. The programs are sponsored by county parks, nature centers, and park reserves to promote environmental awareness. Flannel board stories, puppet shows, bird watching, and animal tracking are used to increase the children's knowledge of nature (Kern, 1982).

Teen suicide prevention. Every year at least 500,000 teenagers attempt suicide, with 5,000 succeeding. Among 15- to 19-year-olds, suicide is now the second leading cause of death. This represents a 300% increase since 1955 (Gelman & Gangelhoff, 1983). Traditional suicide prevention approaches involve the use of therapy and antidepressant drugs. There are over 200 suicide centers nationwide with 24-hour hotlines employing professionals and volunteers. Other treatment programs teach high school students how to deal with sudden catastrophic loss, use cognitive therapy in which patients focus on their current problems through dialogue, or teach coping skills to children. Much of the optimism, however, surrounding suicide prevention is based on the link between depression and suicide, the role of biology in depression, and the discovery of effective drugs that counteract depression.

Psychology and law

Forensic psychology. Forensic psychology is the term given to the applied and clinical facets of psychology and law. Forensic psychology might help a judge decide which parent should have custody of the children or evaluate the victim of an accident to determine if he or she sustained psychological or neurological damage. In criminal cases, forensic psychologists might evaluate a defendant's mental competence to stand trial. Some forensic psychologists counsel inmates and probationers; others counsel the victims of crimes and help them prepare to testify, cope with emotional distress, and resume their normal activities.

Some specialists in this field have doctoral degrees in both psychology and law. Others were trained in a traditional psychology graduate program, such as clinical, counseling, social, or experimental, and chose courses, research topics, and practical experiences to fit their interest in psychology and law.

Jobs for people with doctoral degrees are available in psychology departments, law schools, research organizations, community mental health agencies, law enforcement agencies, courts, and correctional settings. Some forensic psychologists work in private practice. Master's- and bachelor's-level positions are available in prisons, correctional institutions, probation departments, forensic units of mental institutions, law enforcement agencies, and community-based programs that assist victims.

Assisting victims of crime and violence. Until recently, the needs of victims of crime were largely ignored. Now there is widespread recognition of the needs of victims of all crimes, spouses and children of alcoholics, wives of prisoners, battered women, and abused children. Victims may experience posttraumatic stress disorders in which they continue to re-experience their trauma. Symptoms can involve disordered emotions, nightmares, or problems of concentration. The support of family, co-workers, police, and the courts is crucial to the victim's full recovery (Cunningham, 1983).

Treatment programs are rare, and they are scattered. Victims of the Love Canal environmental disaster organized a community-based self-help program to provide information, emotional support, and a sense of control (Wolinsky, 1982). Parents of Murdered Children meets informally in Minneapolis to provide an opportunity for members to talk to others who have had similar experiences (Parsons, 1983). The Governor's Conference on Children of Alcoholics meets in New York to help the children of alcoholic parents (Klemsrud, 1983). And shelters for battered women are becoming more numerous (Piltz, 1977). The Connecticut Prison Association has created a "Women in Crisis" program for the wives and girlfriends of prisoners from Hartford who often cannot get work, housing, or insurance ("Program Helps," 1977).

Profiling for apprehending criminals and selecting juries. Profiling has had widespread application in apprehending criminals. Psychologists are increasingly involved as consultants to law enforcement authorities. Profiling can be used to identify the kind of person likely to commit a class of crimes, such as auto theft or mass murder. Or it can be used to describe the person who actually committed a crime. In either case, the focus is on the criminal rather than the crime. The profiling expert tries to rule out certain candidates and rule in others, thus giving law enforcement officers some idea of the most effective places to look for suspects and suggesting what questions to ask.

More controversial uses of profiling involve jury selections. Psychological experts use readings of nonverbal behavior, body language, and quasi-clinical questions to identify attitudes and values of prospective jury members with the goal of selecting a jury sympathetic to a client's case (Gordon, 1984).

Treating sex offenders. The active treatment of sex offenders is still in the pioneering stage. Although much progress has been made in this field, many challenges remain. Both training and research support need improvement, as well as more support from the criminal justice system and greater public awareness (Fisher, 1984). Programs now typically involve sex education, assertiveness training, and socialization. The work can be stressful, but the potential benefits to society are great.

Moral specialists. The rapid development of modern technologies that have a direct impact on human life has created moral and ethical questions that are difficult to resolve. Technologies for artificial birth, identification of genes that predispose people to certain diseases, life-support devices, and organ transplants raise questions (Otten, 1984). Should a woman who is carrying a deformed fetus have an abortion? What should be done about patients who refuse blood transfusions for religious reasons? These questions are complex and provide a challenge to resolving them. A national institute, The Hastings Center, has been established to explore these questions and to educate others (Otten, 1983).

Those who educate the medical profession in these issues and help people to reach decisions consistent with their moral, ethical, and religious beliefs usually have training in the liberal arts and in workshops conducted by The Hastings Center for medical personnel, lawyers, social scientists, and clergy.

Guidance and counseling

Recruiting organ donors. Cardiologists estimate that as many as 50,000 to 100,000 people who die from heart disease each year could be saved if organs were available. Although there are about 20,000 potential donors each year, only about 2,500 actually donate organs (Schwartz, 1983). There are as many as 110 programs for processing organs nationwide. By 1990, $200 to $400 million a year will be paid to individuals and agencies who can supply organs. Although 6,500 kidneys were supplied by donors in 1983, at least that many people needing transplants were without donors (Waldholz, 1984).

A great need exists for those who can recruit potential donors or persuade families of qualified persons to donate organs. Currently, the North American Transplant Coordinators Organization maintains a 24-hour hotline in an effort to bring donors and patients together. The Organ Procurement Agency of Southern California catalogs needs, solicits organ donations, and coordinates available organs from 300 community hospitals. Currently, the Red Cross intends to become involved in the organ transplant market (Waldholz, 1984).

Profiling for recruitment. As many as 25% of all counties have a shortage of medical personnel. This has caused private firms, hospitals, and communities to recruit medical personnel. Recruiting firms, therefore, could fill a real need by matching the profiles of communities that need doctors with the profiles of eligible doctors. The growing competitiveness among hospitals has caused administrators to view their doctors as their most valuable resource and generators of revenue. Hospital administrators now recruit actively to woo doctors to work at the hospital and to keep them there (Waldholz, 1982). There is evidence that by the next decade profiling could be used to recruit another group of professionals—teachers (Inman, 1984).

Admissions counseling. High schools throughout the nation are graduating fewer and fewer students. To counteract this trend, colleges and universities, especially small colleges, have actively begun to market their product and services, and recruit freshmen. For many colleges and universities, success in recruiting will determine whether they remain open. Although declining enrollments make college administrators uneasy, it is an opportunity for bright, aggressive admissions counselors with skills in working with prospective students. Such work would involve traveling, counseling, advising, evaluating, informing, and processing prospective students ("Letters," 1983).

Counseling people with special needs. A demand exists to help those who do not fit easily into categories that are used for the delivery of human services or who have needs so special that few traditional agencies can help them. Although there are as many as one million homeless, mentally ill people, few mental health personnel want to work with them. Their problems are seen as intractable, and because they have no home address, they are often outside the jurisdictions of social services systems. Some are products of well-meaning deinstitutionalization. Furthermore, many are homeless women who are often victims of abuse. Most missions and other shelters are for men. Society apparently has been slow to respond to these women because they do not pose a threat to anyone.

Little is known about the homeless because many are unwilling or unable to cooperate with authorities. The mentally ill are particularly likely to be among the homeless because they are unwilling or unable to seek help from social service agencies, they have trouble with daily tasks of living, they are vulnerable to stress or change, and they lack skills to maintain a network for support. There is also a need to train the mentally retarded in sheltered workshops, help institutions and agencies redesign ways of doing things to accommodate their needs, and advocate on their behalf.

Posttraumatic stress disorders are known to affect victims of natural disasters, family disasters, and war. Those who have committed or witnessed acts of violence exhibit some of the same symptoms—depression, disorientation, and anxiety. The Veterans Administration developed its Outreach Program for veterans in 1979 and eventually employed some 400 professionals, nonprofessionals, and volunteers in 91 centers. There still exists a need for professionals with experience in working with Vietnam veterans (Schaar, 1980). In addition, the Veterans Administration is planning a large-scale study of posttraumatic stress disorder. Even corporations have become involved in treatment attempts. Corporate programs are needed in other settings to make veterans aware of benefits, educate managers to the special needs of Vietnam veterans, and combat the negative stereotypes that often exist.

Family psychology. Family psychologists are practitioners, researchers, and educators concerned with the prevention of family conflict,

the treatment of marital and family problems, and the maintenance of normal family functioning. They concentrate on the family structure and the interaction between members rather than on the individual.

As service providers, they often design and conduct programs for marital enrichment, premarital preparation, improved parent–child relations, and parent education about children with special needs. They also provide treatment for marital conflicts and problems that affect whole families.

As researchers, they seek to identify environmental and personal factors that are associated with improved family functioning. They may study communication patterns in families with a hyperactive child or conduct research on child abuse or the effects of divorce and remarriage on family members. A subgroup of family psychologists specializes in the prevention and treatment of sexual dysfunction and in research on human sexuality.

Doctoral programs in family psychology are just beginning to appear. Traditionally, most family psychologists have earned their degree in a professional area of psychology and then obtained advanced training in departments of psychiatry, family institutes, or through individual supervision. Postdoctoral training programs are becoming more common.

Family psychologists are often employed in medical schools, hospitals, private practice, family institutes, and community agencies. Job opportunities also exist for university teachers, forensic family psychologists, and consultants to industry.

Psychology of women

The psychology of women is the study of psychological and social factors affecting women's development and behavior. The field includes the study of stereotypes about women, the relation of hormones to behavior, women's achievements in mathematics and science, the development of gender roles and identity, sexuality, psychological problems of women and their treatment, and physical and sexual abuse of women and girls.

Psychologists focusing in the psychology of women are found in academic settings and a variety of clinical settings. Current research topics include women's reactions to being raped and the best treatment techniques for rape victims, factors that promote managerial success, factors that discourage talented women from obtaining advanced mathematics training, and the causes of eating disorders such as anorexia. Clinicians whose area of concentration is the psychology of women may practice feminist therapy with women and girls.

Most psychologists whose concern is the psychology of women have received their training in clinical, developmental, or social psychology, or in psychobiology, pursuing their special interest within these broader areas. Teaching positions for doctoral-level psychologists are available in psychology and women's studies departments. Researchers who focus on health issues for women have been hired as faculty members in nursing, public health, social work, or psychiatry departments of universities. Clinicians work in mental health centers and in private practice.

Psychology and aging

Researchers in the psychology of aging (geropsychology) draw on sociology, biology, and other disciplines as well as psychology to study the factors associated with adult development and aging. For example, they may investigate how the brain and the nervous system change as humans age and what effects those changes have on behavior or how a person's style of coping with problems varies with age. Clinicians in geropsychology apply their knowledge about the aging process to improve the psychological welfare of the elderly.

Many people interested in the psychology of aging are trained in a more traditional graduate program in psychology, such as experimental, clinical, developmental, or social. While they are enrolled in such a program, they become geropsychologists by focusing their research, coursework, and practical experiences on adult development and aging.

Increases in the percentage of the population that is aged 65 or over and greater social attention to the needs, the problems, and the potentials of older persons have contributed to a growth in the demand for geropsychologists. Geropsychologists are finding jobs in academic settings, research centers, industry, health care organizations, mental health clinics, and agencies serving the elderly. Some are engaged in private practice, either as clinical or counseling psychologists, or as consultants on such matters as the design and the evaluation of programs.

A doctorate is normally required for teaching, research, and clinical practice, but an increasing number of employment opportunities are becoming available for people with associate, bachelor's, and master's degrees. These positions typically involve the supervised provision of services to adults in nursing homes, senior citizens centers, or state and local government offices for the elderly.

References

Bazar, J. (1980, February). Behavioral medicine meeting covers old and new ground. *APA Monitor,* p. 8.

Bishop, J. (1983, December 23). New gene probes may permit early predictions of disease. *The Wall Street Journal,* p. 11.

Cordes, C. (1984, May). Teaching students to learn can make excellence happen. *APA Monitor,* p. 19.

Cunningham, S. (1983, May). Crime victims: New research spurred by belated recognition of psychological component. *APA Monitor,* pp. 3, 24-25.

Cunningham, S. (1984, February). Gifted battle myth to gain support for programs. *APA Monitor,* pp. 20-22.

Doctors treat minds as well as bodies of their tiny patients. (1977, October 11). *The Free Press,* p. 20.

Fisher, K. (1984, May). Old attitudes slow treatment gains of sex offenders. *APA Monitor,* pp. 23-24.

Freeman, M. (1980, April). Biofeedback Institute: Struggling with professional issues despite public acceptance. *APA Monitor,* p. 10.

Gaiter, D. J. (1984, January 15). Animal welfare part of school curriculum. *Minneapolis Tribune.*

Gelman, D., & Gangelhoff, B. K. (1983, August 15). Teen-age suicide in the sun belt. *Newsweek,* pp. 70, 72, 74.

Gordon, R. (1984, February). The art and science of jury selection (ad). *APA Monitor,* p. 12.

Hunt, A. R. (1984, August 21). Campaigning in the family way. *The Wall Street Journal.*

Inman, V. (1984, January). Certification of teachers lacking courses in education stirs battles in several states. *The Wall Street Journal,* p. 1.

Kern, B. (1982, April 11). Parks put kids in touch with nature. *Minneapolis Tribune.*

Klemsrud, J. (1983). Conference hears pleas for helping children share anguish, learn to cope. *Minneapolis Tribune.*

Letters, applications, transcripts: If it's hectic this must be admissions. (1983, July). *MSU Today.*

Lublin, J. S. (1984, May 24). After-school projects proliferate for children of working parents. *The Wall Street Journal,* pp. 1, 24.

McCrary, E. (1983, May 29). N.C. hospitals stress role as wellness centers. *Minneapolis Tribune.*

Otten, A. (1983, November 23). As medicine advances, Hastings Center tries to solve ethical issues. *The Wall Street Journal,* pp. 1, 18.

Otten, A. (1984, August 27). Infertility enterprises give birth to concern. *The Wall Street Journal,* p. 10.

Parsons, J. (1983, October 30). Parents of murdered children share anguish, learn to cope. *Minneapolis Tribune.*

Piltz, B. (1977, March 29). Mankato officials address wife-beating problem. *MSU Independent,* pp. 1, 4.

Program helps family, friends of prisoners. (1977, December 12). *Minneapolis Tribune,* p. 6EX.

Schaar, K. (1980, December). Vietnam veteran counseling sites face uncertainty but seek staff. *APA Monitor.*

Schellhardt, T. D. (1983, May 4). Officials fight to let elderly keep pets in federally assisted housing. *The Wall Street Journal.*

Schwartz, H. (1983, July 25). Providing incentives for organ donors. *The Wall Street Journal*, p. 8.

Waldholz, M. (1982, December 29). To keep doors open, nonprofit hospitals act like businesses. *The Wall Street Journal*, p. 1.

Waldholz, M. (1984, August 8). Red Cross's plan to procure organs could hurt smaller organizations. *The Wall Street Journal*, p. 29.

Watson, C. (1983, January 30). Agoraphobia: Fear that keeps people at home. *Minneapolis Tribune*, pp. 1E, 8E-10E.

Wolinsky, J. (1982, December). Self-help group was key for Love Canal residents. *APA Monitor*, p. 31.

Chapter 12

Occupational trends of psychology majors

T his chapter presents the results of several studies. The findings presented in Table 12–1 show the percentages of men and women psychology graduates from Western Illinois University in each of 9 occupational categories. The table offers a comparison of the types of occupations held by these graduates over a 20-year period (1964-1984). Figure 12–1 shows the number of students majoring in psychology at a small midwestern liberal arts college during a 30-year period (1954-1983). Figures 2–4 show some of the trends revealed by that group of psychology majors. Although these findings pertain only to small samples, the general occupational trends revealed are valid. By observing such trends, you can discover for yourself what employment opportunities there are, what graduates have done in the past, and what graduates are doing now.

Table 12–1 presents the findings of surveys conducted in 1977, 1979, and 1984, of psychology majors who graduated from Western Illinois University. Each of the 3 surveys included all psychology majors to that date. The psychology department there was founded in 1961, and the university's first psychology majors graduated in 1964. Thus, the findings of the 1984 survey represent 20 years of psychology graduates. The percentages of respondents to each survey were small (unknown for 1977, 31% for 1979, 17% for 1984). However, the percentages of graduates in each occupational category remains fairly constant.

The data present some interesting findings. For instance, the largest occupational category is human services, which is the most consistent from survey to survey and most balanced between men and women. From 1977 to 1984, there was a dramatic decline, however in the percentage of women holding education jobs and a large increase in the percentage of women enrolled full-time in graduate study.

Material for this chapter was contributed by Frank E. Fulkerson, Western Illinois University; Robert S. Harper, Knox College; Gene F. Smith, Western Illinois University; and Paula Sachs Wise, Western Illinois University.

TABLE 12-1 **Occupational Trends of Western Illinois University Psychology Graduates**

	1977			1979			1984		
	% men	% women	% total	% men	% women	% total	% men	% women	% total
Human services counselors therapists social workers	30.0	30.2	30.0	31.0	30.0	30.6	34.6	34.4	34.5
Education teachers professors school psychologists	11.4	37.2	21.2	15.1	24.3	18.6	12.3	18.3	15.5
Management	10.0	4.7	8.0	14.2	15.7	14.8	18.5	9.7	13.8
Sales stockbrokers insurance agents sales representatives	27.1	2.3	17.7	14.2	2.9	9.8	11.1	2.2	6.3
Graduate school	8.6	4.7	7.1	10.6	11.4	10.9	6.2	17.2	12.1
Professional trades mail carriers police officers construction workers	12.9	4.7	9.7	10.6	2.9	7.7	9.9	4.3	6.9
Clerical secretaries cashiers bank tellers	0.0	7.0	2.7	0.9	11.4	4.9	4.9	8.6	6.9
Miscellaneous/ self-employed	0.0	2.3	0.9	3.5	0.0	2.2	2.5	2.2	2.3
Unemployed	0.0	7.0	2.7	0.0	1.4	0.5	0.0	3.2	1.7

Note: Respondents to 1977 survey include all psychology graduates from 1964 to 1977; respondents to 1979 survey include all from 1964 to 1979; respondents to 1984 survey from 1964 to 1984. Percentages represent totals of all respondents in the survey year.

There was also a steady increase in the percentage of men employed in management positions and a large drop in the percentage of men involved in sales.

Psychology majors have undertaken and continue to go into a variety of jobs, as shown in Table 12–1. Will you be able to get a job with a degree in psychology? Most definitely yes! And as Table 12–1 shows, the types of jobs people obtain with a psychology degree are quite varied. Remember, just as the field of psychology is people-oriented, so too is the world of work.

Now take a look at Figures 1–5. These figures review the 30-year history of psychology majors from a small midwestern liberal arts college. This study was carried out by group-ing all of the graduates into 5-year units, beginning with the majors graduating in June 1954 to those graduating in June 1983. What are the occupational trends of psychology majors over the last 30 years derived from this study? By comparing the figures, you can reach some interesting conclusions.

As Figure 12–1 and 12–2 together show, although the overall number of psychology majors has dropped since the early 1970s, the number of women psychology majors has significantly increased in the past 10 years. This points out that (a) the number of psychology majors has almost doubled over the past 30 years, and (b) the majority of those majors are now women! When you compare Figures 12–1 and 12–3, you find that although the number

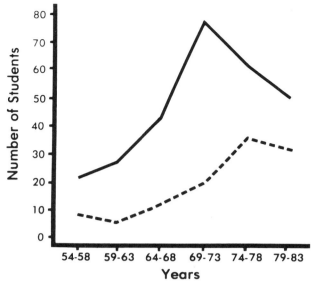

Figure 12−1. The number of students majoring in psychology at a small midwestern liberal arts college. The numbers are grouped in 5-year units from 1954 to 1983. The solid line represents the total number of students; the dotted line represents the number of women psychology majors only.

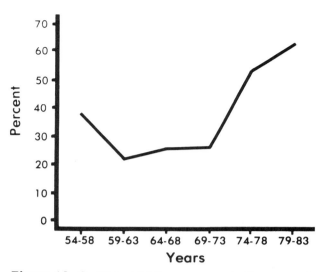

Figure 12−2. The solid line represents the percentages for all women psychology majors from the same midwestern college, grouped similarly in 5-year units from 1954 to 1983.

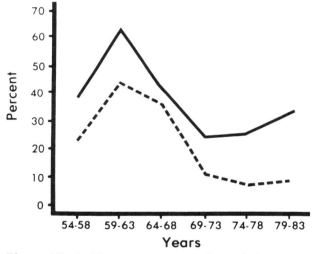

Figure 12−3. The percentage of all psychology majors who continued on to graduate school. The solid line represents those psychology majors who went on to any graduate program; the dotted line represents those who went on to a graduate program in psychology.

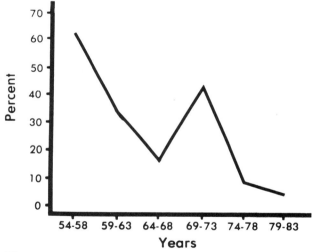

Figure 12−4. The solid line represents the percentage of all women psychology graduates of the small midwestern college who married soon after graduation, grouped in 5-year units from 1954 to 1983.

of psychology majors who have gone on to graduate school has not declined significantly in 30 years, the percentage of graduates who majored in psychology and went on to graduate school immediately after college has declined greatly in the past 20 years. Therefore, (a) about 33% of psychology graduates eventually enter graduate school in some field, and (b) only about 10% of those enter graduate school in psychology.

Figure 12−4 shows the percentage of all women psychology graduates who immediately married after graduation. Except for one upswing, the figure shows an overall decline. Women are now less likely to marry after graduation. By looking at Figure 12−5, you can see that the majority of psychology graduates are going into the nonacademic workforce and are entering the workforce in positions that do not derive directly from their majors!

Psychology majors in the workplace 67

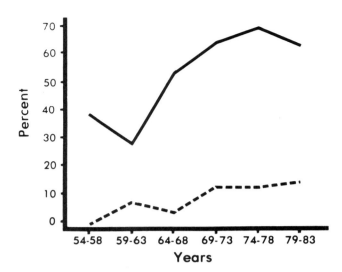

Figure 12—5. The percentage of psychology majors who took jobs after graduation. The solid line represents the percentage of those who took any job; the dotted line represents those who took psychology-related jobs.

PART 4

Presenting yourself to employers

Chapter 13

The résumé, cover letter, and interview

Before you ever begin to seek a job actively, whether or not you are still in college, there are a few things you should know order to conduct a successful job search. You probably already know many of these things through career guidance books or counselors. Nevertheless, it is necessary to consider them again in more detail. They are an essential part of the job-hunting process.

Your résumé and cover letter provide a way for you to present yourself, your background, and your qualifications to a potential employer. If that employer likes what he or she sees, you may be asked to come in for an interview, which is your best opportunity to show who you are and to demonstrate your poise and ability—in person! And afterwards, you should send along a follow-up, to thank that employer for the interview and to express your interest in the job again.

When seeking a job, you are going to have to prepare yourself for these presentations. How well you prepare for these will determine your success in seeking a job. How you go about preparing for these is the point of this chapter. The quality of these presentations is critical. So here are some helpful hints.

The résumé

Your résumé should provide a brief sketch of your background and qualifications aimed at eliciting an employer's interest in you as a potential employee. The résumé should include your name, address, a telephone number where you can be reached, and the facts of your education and previous employment. Pertinent extracurricular activities, honors, awards, and interests should also be included.

Take a look at Sample Résumé 13–1 to see how the facts of a résumé can be handled. All of the information that this applicant wants to express is broken down into logical, prominently displayed categories. Each activity within the categories is preceded by its date

Material for this chapter was contributed by Bruce R. Fretz, University of Maryland.

and a concise statement of what the activity involved. Because the applicant in this example is a college student who lacks significant work experience, he has decided to highlight his education by ordering it first. If you also lack sufficient work experience, this may be the way for you to proceed in developing your own résumé.

Under the category of Work Experience, the applicant has provided dates for each job he has had together with a brief description. The description should be as concise as possible and should try to show not only responsibilities and duties but accomplishments if any. Additional categories, such as Extracurricular Activities and Honors and Awards, should lend support to your educational and work experiences as well as to illustrate that you are well-rounded, active, and motivated.

If you wish, you may state your career objective at the beginning of the résumé. A career-objective statement can show an employer your career focus. References, however, need not be written on the résumé itself. These can be provided separately upon request. Simply state at the close of your résumé, "References available upon request."

Now take a look at Sample Résumé 13—2. Notice how this applicant has provided supplemental information that supports her educational experience. In this example, this type of information is valuable to highlight because it has a direct bearing on her career objective. In addition, she has provided a special skills section in her résumé that points out potentially valuable skills that could be seen by an employer as useful.

Remember that your résumé is your calling card. It should present your background, qualifications, and accomplishments. Keep an up-to-date list, with addresses and telephone numbers, of five or more faculty members or

Sample Résumé 13—1

William Ingloff
408 Haberside Drive
Largo, FL 33540
(803) 365-7843

CAREER OBJECTIVE	Copywriting for an advertising firm, for which strong research skills would be essential assets
EDUCATION	
1986	University of Missouri, Columbia BA in Psychology, minors in Journalism, Advertising
WORK EXPERIENCE	
Summer 1985	Provided research assistance for major statistical study on critical color variables in men's clothing preferences, conducted by Prof. James Marks, Department of Psychology, University of Missouri
1984–1985	Worked as Review Assistant for introductory psychology course, collecting and grading standardized tests, providing general assistance for professor and staff, Department of Psychology, University of Missouri
1983–1984	Bank Teller, Columbia Federal Savings & Loan
EXTRACURRICULAR ACTIVITIES	
1985–present	Volunteer tutor at emotionally disturbed children's home
1983–present	Advertising editor, campus newspaper
HONORS AND AWARDS	
1978	Phi Kappa Phi (Senior Honor Society)
1977	Psi Chi (Psychology Honor Society)

References available upon request

previous employers whom you know well and who would provide favorable references. If and when an employer wants to verify the facts or receive additional comment or information about your work or character, that employer will ask for references to check. For a college recruiter, you may supply a few references when submitting your résumé. Always keep a copy of your reference list handy, along with additional copies of your résumé.

You should try to keep your résumé to one page. It should be neat and accurately typed. If you are applying for several different kinds of positions, you may want to prepare a different résumé for each type of position, especially if you have a different career objective for each. If this is the case, consider removing your career-objective statement from your résumé and incorporating it in your cover letter. In that way, you may not have to rewrite your résumé each time you apply for a different job. In addition, you may wish to consider, as an alternative to a traditional résumé, the more demanding but potentially more valuable Qualifications Brief, which is discussed in chapter 14.

Sample Cover Letter 13—2

Jacqueline S. Connors
37 Brookside Drive
Northampton, MA 01060

June 4, 1986

Mr. John Smith
Child Care Emporium
100 Main Street
Northampton, MA 01060

Dear Mr. Smith:

As a recent graduate of Smith College, I have gained valuable knowledge and experience in the areas of child development and education. As my enclosed resume shows, my psychology degree program emphasized developmental psychology, family relations, and childhood education. In addition, I have worked closely with underprivileged and handicapped children in recreational settings. I also am fluent in conversational Spanish.

I would appreciate the opportunity to apply for your posted position for Child Care Specialist. The job description is in line with my career objective. I believe I have the necessary background and qualifications for the position, and I am sure I could make a positive contribution to your agency as a child care provider.

I would like to talk to you further about my qualifications and what the position entails. If you would like to schedule an interview, please call at (413) 257-8195.

I look forward to meeting with you.

Sincerely,

Jacqueline S. Connors

The cover letter

A cover letter should always accompany your résumé. It should be as specific and as concise as possible. The letter need not tell much about you, but it should highlight those aspects in your résumé that pertain to the position for which you are applying. In short, your cover letter should not only introduce but also complement your résumé.

The cover letter should refer to the specific position for which you are applying. You may wish to briefly state how the position fits with your career objective. The cover letter should convey your interest in the position you want, as well as your interest in and knowledge of the organization itself. The letter should be designed to direct the employer to those points in your résumé that relate to the tasks of the position you want. And as with any letter, be sure to include a mailing address and telephone number where you can be reached.

The interview

The employment interview is the most important event in your job search. Your résumé and cover letter are, in fact, merely tools to use to get an interview. The interview is your best and only opportunity to demonstrate that you are the right person for the job.

How you present yourself depends on how well you prepare yourself in advance. Interviewers are continually amazed at the number of applicants who drift into job interviews without any apparent preparation and only the vaguest idea of what they are going to say. Their manner says, "Well, here I am," and that is often the end of it in more ways than one! Others create an impression of indifference by

Sample Résumé 13—2

Jacqueline S. Connors
37 Brookside Drive
Northampton, MA 01060
(413) 257-8195

CAREER OBJECTIVE   Child care specialist, requiring a knowledge and
background in child development and education

EDUCATION

1986   Smith College, Northampton, MA
BA in Psychology, minors in Human Development,
Music

(Focus of psychology program on developmental
psychology, supplemented by courses in family
relations, early childhood education, and art for
children)

EXPERIENCE

Summer 1985   Assisted as intern assistant to coordinator of
Schenectady Family Services Program for summer
educational and recreational services for
underprivileged children

Summer 1984   Worked as camp counselor for handicapped children,
Camp Adirondac

1983–1984   Tutored four children ages 8 to 10 during academic
year to help in their development of vital educational
skills

1985–1986   Worked as review assistant for introductory child
psychology course, collecting and grading multiple-
choice tests and offering general assistance, Smith
College

EXTRACURRICULAR ACTIVITIES

1983–1985   Smith College Choir
1983–1984   Field hockey team

HONORS AND AWARDS

1984–1985   Psi Chi (Psychology Honor Society), vice president

SPECIAL SKILLS

Certified American National Red Cross Life Saving and Water Safety Instructor

Fluent in conversational Spanish

References available upon request

acting too casual. And there are others who work themselves into a frenzy and arrive at an interview in the last stages of nervous fright, unable to do much more than gulp and answer questions in monosyllables. In such cases, it is important to realize that the interviewer is human too, and often a very pleasant person. Moreover, the responsibility rests on you and you alone to project yourself in an enthusiastic, positive manner, to appear competitive.

Prior to your interview, it is imperative to do some research on the organization you are interviewing with. You will want to know what type of positions and programs the organization has. You will also want information about the organization such as size, locations, services, products, and so forth. This will give you some background information and provide material for you to form questions to ask. Sources of company information are available in most libraries. Ask your librarian for help.

It is difficult to actually rehearse your role in an upcoming interview. It is best to rely on your own courtesy and good sense. Some practice interviewing with friends may increase your confidence. There are, however, some basic rules and situations common to many interviews that may help you. For instance, be on time, dress neatly and appropriately, and act businesslike.

Before you have your interview, you should know the correct pronunciation of the interviewer's name. Be prepared for at least one surprise question right at the start, such as "What can I do for you?," "Tell me about yourself," or "Why are you interested in this organization?" If you think those are easy questions to answer without some previous thought, just try it! Preparation counts.

If the interviewer wants to know what he or she can do for you, say that you would like a job in a certain operation of the organization, with the idea of advancing. Or say anything that will show your interest in progress with the organization. Be as specific as you can. If you are asked to talk about yourself, express those things that you feel relate to the particular job for which you are applying. Learn to articulate your personal strengths and assets. Be informative without boasting or relating your troubles. If you are asked to discuss your strengths and weaknesses, best and worst qualities, keep your answers business related and positive. Try to show the "silver lining" in references to your faults. Should the interviewer ask why you are interested in the organization, if you have studied the organization's background and information, you will not be at a loss for words.

During the interview, look the interviewer

directly in the eye, and continue to do so from time to time. This is important. Nearly every interviewer is conscious of it. Remember to smile frequently, at appropriate occasions. Some interviewers like to do most of the talking during the interview. They prefer to judge you by your reactions, such as the interest, comprehension, and intelligence you demonstrate. Others hardly speak at all. Here it will prove especially valuable for you to have rehearsed your answers to typical questions and to have composed several of your own questions for the interviewer regarding the job and the company.

If at some time during the interview you get the impression that it is not going well, don't let your discouragement show. You have nothing to lose and maybe much to gain by continuing confidently. The last few minutes often change things. Once in a great while an interviewer who is genuinely interested in your possibilities may seem to discourage you to test your reaction. If you remain confident and determined, you will probably make a good impression.

In your answers to questions, make sure that your good points get across. They won't become apparent unless you discuss them, but avoid sounding conceited. It is best to offer brief, factual examples of your accomplishments that somehow relate to the position for which you are interviewing. For example, saying "I paid for 75% of my college expenses by working part-time" can demonstrate your drive compared with merely stating, "I am a hard worker and I want to get ahead."

As with any job search, you are bound to have many job interviews. Over time you will find that most interviews will consist of simple questions and answers. Your ability to answer quickly and intelligently is important. If your answers are confused and contradictory, you could find yourself in trouble. The best way to prevent contradictory answers is to speak the plain truth. A frank answer, even if it seems a little unfavorable to you, is better than an exaggeration that may tangle you up.

In any interview you have, conduct yourself as if you are determined to get the job you are discussing. Always show an interest in the specifics of the job by sharing any knowledge you may have about the type of work involved and by asking questions. Avoid giving the impression that you are not yet sure what you want. Don't say, "I'll do anything if I'm given the chance to learn," or "I don't know what I want to do; I hope that you can suggest something." Whenever possible, apply for a specific job or field of work. If there is no opening in the line you suggest, the way you present what you have to offer may lead the interviewer to suggest another job or department, perhaps even better than the one you were seeking.

Near the completion of the interview, try to determine when you will be notified of a decision, and if the interviewer doesn't indicate when you will be notified, ask if you may call in a week or two. Don't be too discouraged if no definite offer is made or no specific salary is discussed. Many employment application forms that you are required to fill out before being interviewed will ask you to state the minimum salary you will accept. You should try to ascertain in advance the salary range for the particular job.

Upon leaving, remember to thank the interviewer for his or her time. If for some reason you feel the interview did not go well, remember that interviewers, companies, and jobs differ greatly. You will learn much from interview to interview, and you will certainly do better in successive ones. The important thing is to keep trying.

The follow-up

Following up after an interview is essential. Any verbal or phone arrangements you make with an employer before, during, or after the interview should be followed by a letter. After

---

The following is a list of frequently asked interview questions. Get to know them. Work out clear and concise answers to them before your interview. You can greatly enhance your chances for employment by doing so.

- Why do you think you might like to work for our company?
- In what type of position are you most interested?
- What jobs have you held? How were they obtained and why did you leave?
- What are your future career plans?
- In what school activities have you participated? Why? Which did you enjoy the most? What extracurricular offices have you held?
- How do you spend your spare time? What are your hobbies?
- What courses did you like the best? Least? Why?
- Why did you choose your particular field of work?
- What percentage of your college expenses did you earn? How?
- How did you spend your vacations while in school?
- Do you feel that you have received a good general training?

- What qualifications do you have that make you feel that you will be successful in your field?
- What do you think determines an employee's progress in a good company?
- What personal characteristics do you think are necessary for success in your chosen field?
- What have you learned from some of the jobs you have held?
- What was your record in military service (if applicable)?
- Are you willing to relocate or travel for company business?
- What jobs have you enjoyed the most? Least? Why?
- What do you consider to be your strengths and weaknesses insofar as your job knowledge and skills are concerned?
- What are the challenges of your chosen field?

the interview, you should write a brief note to thank the interviewer, again expressing your appreciation for his or her consideration and expressing your interest in the organization. If you do not receive word on your status within the amount of time that was indicated, call or write the interviewer asking if a decision has been made. In such a letter, you might take a sentence or two to review your abilities in relation to the employer's needs.

When you eventually receive an offer of a position, acknowledge the offer in writing, express your appreciation for the offer, and give the date by which you will advise them of your decision (if you have other pending job offers you wish to consider before making your choice). When declining an offer, always be polite; one day you may want to be considered again by that employer.

Chapter 14

The qualifications brief

As explained in chapter 12, a résumé has two primary functions. It can show an employer an applicant's identity and qualifications, and it can encourage that employer to interview the applicant. The traditional, chronological résumé often does not work effectively, however, because of its usual emphasis on listing experiences and education with little elaboration of abilities and qualifications.

An alternative to the traditional résumé is the qualifications brief, or functional résumé, which stresses qualifications, accomplishments, and abilities in a functional rather than a chronological format. The qualifications brief was first developed by Richard Lathrop in his two books, *Who's Hiring Who* and *Don't Use a Résumé*. These books are valuable job-hunting guides. These and other valuable resource books are listed in chapter 23. Every college student and would-be job hunter should be familiar with these.

Writing an effective qualifications brief requires a good deal of time and energy. The task can help bring your career goals into perspective (at least for the immediate future) and result in a concise description of abilities, qualifications, education, and experience to support them. Successful job hunters know that they must tailor themselves to an employer's needs. Writing a qualifications brief is a first step in becoming a success.

Therefore, three questions face you as a psychology major when writing your first qualifications brief.

1. What is your career objective?

2. What qualifications support your objective?

3. What is the most effective way to organize this information?

Material for this chapter was contributed by Vicki M. Wilson, Hospital Commission, Olympia, WA.

Presenting yourself to employers   79

Step 1: clarifying your career objective

Your career objective is a concise statement of your career goals and qualifications and how they can functionally serve an employer. As a psychology major with a liberal arts background, your objective would be to clarify your direction. Psychology graduates are qualified for any number of entry-level positions in the workforce depending on their interests, the type of psychology courses taken, and any supplementary coursework. Simply stating that you have a psychology degree provides little information about you to an employer.

Before writing your career objective, you first need to clarify what you want to do and where you want to do it. For example, a typical statement among psychology majors is "I want to work with people." Does this mean individual, vocational, academic, rehabilitative, or parole counseling? Would the counseling be with normal, mentally retarded, emotionally immature, or physically disabled people, and would they be children, adolescents, or adults? Would the desired location be a community mental health center, hospital, group home, or school? Would the goal be to instruct, supervise, persuade, or serve? Are you more interested in working with information or things than with people? You must be able to answer all of these questions before starting to write your objective.

Fortunately, there are many resources you can turn to for help in answering these questions. Several valuable reference books are listed in chapter 23. These books will help you gain a sense of yourself and your place in the world of work. As a prospective job seeker, you should become familiar with these books and others like them. Look for them in your college or local library.

Browsing through federal, state, and local job listings, as well as the Yellow Pages, can also be helpful. Consult with the staff of your college Career Placement Center (see chapter 7) or professors of the psychology department about your questions. Read through pamphlets printed by professional organizations, such as the American Society for Training and Development and the American Psychological Association, for information on the types of agencies and jobs in which psychology graduates most often enter.

You can also find out more about occupations through informational interviewing. As referred to in chapter 7, informational interviewing consists of talking with people who have jobs similar to those you think you might be interested in. Friends, relatives, placement

counselors, and department advisors can help locate willing volunteers. Also, your college Career Placement Center may have the names and telephone numbers of alumni who have volunteered to talk to students about what they do in the professional world.

To arrange informational interviews, speak to those people you have selected to talk to and explain that you are researching occupations. Emphasize that you are not seeking employment. Write out a list of questions before the interview. Useful questions might include the following:

- What is your typical work day like? Your typical work week?
- What type of background is necessary for your position?
- What education and experience do you have?
- What do you like most about what you do? Least?
- What rewards come with your position?
- What advice do you have for someone wanting to enter this field?

Volunteer work, internships, summer jobs, and fieldwork for credit also provide excellent opportunities for exploring careers. Attending local meetings of professional organizations can also help you learn about occupations, make contacts, and do some informational interviewing.

Having clarified what you want to do and where you want to do it, the first step in writing an effective qualifications brief is almost complete. The final element involves stating your career objective. Your career objective should be a concise, one-sentence description of an immediate, short-range objective. It should be stated in terms of your abilities and accomplishments as supported by your education and experience to date. Since the purpose of the qualifications brief is to convince an employer of your suitability, it should be written in line with the employer's goals and should stress what you have to offer, not what you want. Job titles should not be mentioned. Doing so would only limit your job possibilities.

The following are some examples of career objectives:

- Hospital public relations, for which knowledge of procedures and problems, oral and written expertise, and ability to work with the public will be assets.

- Social service research, requiring strong practical computer, statistics, research design, and program evaluation skills.

- Recreational therapy with people who have physical disabilities, for which program development, communication, and broad sports and crafts skills can help maximize agency goals.

Any one of these career objectives could be that of a psychology major looking for a first job. Each objective is based on personal experience and interests, courses used to supplement the psychology degree, and related volunteer work.

To summarize, an effective objective should (a) be a concise, clear statement of a desired job, (b) include your primary abilities and accomplishments as supported by your experience and education, (c) avoid job titles, and (d) stress what you can do for an employer.

Step 2: supporting your career objective

Once you have written your career objective, you need to back it up with a description of your qualifications, accomplishments, experience, and a brief summary of your education. The worksheet provided in this chapter may help you to clarify which of your qualifications best support your objective and aid you in describing your qualifications in writing.

Step 3: writing your qualifications brief

Now that you have written down your career objective and supporting information, your next step is to organize your supporting information effectively in a functional format. Here begins the process of forming your qualifications brief. Although the functional format is generally the most effective for the less-experienced college student or graduate, no one style fits everyone. If another format, such as the traditional résumé of chapter 13, will better showcase your qualifications, you should use it.

Strengths. Carefully review your worksheet entries, especially your answers to those questions involving skills, abilities, and accomplishments based on your previous job experience. Review those skills acquired through your education and personal experiences as well. From these, what do you believe to be your strongest skill, ability, accomplishment, or experience, and how does it support your career objective? What is your second strongest? Third strongest? Select up to four strengths you believe are relevant to your career objective, and on a separate sheet of paper make them headings for the qualifications brief. Locate those strengths that you believe best support your ability to work for an employer.

The aim of this is to create an image of a person best qualified to meet an employer's needs. You might start with the most qualifying experience (not necessarily the most recent) that supports the employer's needs, then continue with the next best, and so on. You might alternately decide that skill headings (for example, interviewing, writing, and public speaking, or some other combination) may better represent you to an employer.

After each strength heading, describe what form that strength has taken and how it is relevant to the employer's needs. Such a description can range from a paragraph to individual sentences with bullets. Use simple, direct language. Cite examples of your successes and even praise given to you by other employers or teachers. Try to portray the scope and effect of your work, accomplishments, the abilities you have gained and used, and the results you have produced.

Look at the Sample Qualifications Brief (page 83). Here the applicant has chosen three strengths that she believes can best support her career objective. Under each she has highlighted not only the activities or work associated with each, but the insights she gained and praise she received for her work. Rather than just listing her duties, the applicant has tied activities to accomplishments and results. Not only did she work, but she produced positive, effective results because of her work!

Under the first strength heading, for instance, the applicant refers to an evaluation she conducted for teens with physical disabilities, which is followed by a description of a survey she developed that resulted in new programs being started. And she finished the category by offering evidence of her success. Each activity she lists is supported in turn by a positive accomplishment that was beneficial to her employer. Note how the applicant has subordinated the place and date of her employment. Compared to her accomplishments,

---

Sample Résumé 14—1

Sandra F. Johnson
4200 East Elroy
Seattle, WA 98167
(206) 982-0417

CAREER OBJECTIVE	Recreational therapist for people with physical disabilities
EDUCATION	
1984	University of Washington BA Psychology
WORK EXPERIENCE	
1983–1984	Research Assistant, Seattle Park District Conducted evaluation and survey of recreational programs for teens with physical disabilities.
1982–1983	Assistant, Seattle Handicapped Citizens Center Worked in center for adults with physical disabilities, initiated daily sports and craft activities.
1982	Coach, Harborview Rehabilitation Unit Coached swimming, wheelchair basketball, and track and field to young adults; taught crafts, painting, and drawing to newly disabled children in hospital rehabilitation center.
HONORS AND AWARDS	
1984	Scholarship, Seattle Handicapped Citizens Center

---

these are of less importance. Remember, let your qualifications brief showcase your strengths and abilities, not just your previous work experience.

For purposes of comparison, take a moment to compare the Sample Qualifications Brief with the Sample Résumé 14—1. Notice how the brief stresses the applicant's abilities and achievements as opposed to duties. Notice how the Qualifications Brief allows the applicant to emphasize her accomplishments through her work rather than her education. What an employer reads in a Qualifications Brief is work experience and achievement; in a résumé, education and a list of past and present jobs. The Qualifications Brief can provide a more vital, exciting format to showcase your talent.

Education. Your educational information should be placed wherever it will be most effective in your qualifications brief. In some instances, your education may be the most qualifying experience for a particular job, and thus should be listed first to catch an employer's attention. However, when your psy-

chology background is not directly related to the career objective, list your educational credits near the end of your brief. If supplementary coursework or experience is directly related to a given job, indicate how and place it early and prominently in your brief. Professional information, such as memberships in organizations and lists of publications or presentations, if relevant, are best included near the end of the qualifications brief. However, when such items are a major contribution, they may deserve a separate heading altogether.

Personal. This section should close out the brief. Concise sentences can further demonstrate your personality and attitude. Try to end your qualifications brief on a note that makes an employer say, "I want to meet this person."

Fine tuning your qualifications brief

Employers have different needs. Thus changing your career objective to address different employers' needs requires changing your qualifications brief. The changes may require sim-

Sample Qualifications Brief

Sandra F. Johnson
4200 East Elroy
Seattle, WA 98167
(206) 982-0417

OBJECTIVE   Recreational therapy with people who have disabilities, for which program development, interpersonal communication, and broad sports and craft skills can help enhance programs goals.

STRENGTHS

Program Evaluation and Development
- Conducted evaluation of recreational programs for teens with physical disabilities.
- Developed survey that resulted in new programs to increase skills, encourage self-sufficiency, and maximize participants' enjoyment.
- Waiting lists and letters of appreciation confirm program success.

Seattle Park District
August 1983–August 1984

Interpersonal Communication Skills
- Gained insight into needs and problems through work in a center for adults with physical disabilities.
- Initiated daily sports and crafts activities to enhance interest in self and others.
- Staff praised my ability to involve even the most reclusive clients.

Seattle Handicapped Citizens Center
September 1982–June 1983

Sports and Craft Skills
- Active interests in coaching and teaching as a result of participation in many sports, including swimming, basketball, and track and field.
- Lastest coaching effort, wheelchair basketball team, has resulted in increased participation and demand for additional team sports.
- Shared craft skills such as knot tying, painting, and drawing with newly disabled children in hospital rehabilitation center.
- Children, parents, and staff enthusiastically welcomed these activities.

Harborview Rehabilitation Unit
April 1982–June 1982

EDUCATION   BA Psychology, Recreation Supplement
University of Washington, August 1984

Scholarship awarded by Seattle Handicapped Citizens Center

PERSONAL   • Summer and part-time jobs paid 60% of college expenses.
- Believe in maximizing self and others; trust in positive effects of sports and crafts.

ply rewording the career objective or changing the emphasis of the entire brief and selecting new headings. Such changes will be much easier if you keep your job, education, and personal experience descriptions up-to-date.

The final version of your qualifications brief should be one page. No matter how extensive your background, if the crucial information cannot be read quickly, most employers won't be interested. No matter how well you write, have a friend, counselor, or relative look at your finished brief for any misspelled words, grammatical errors, or unclear meanings. A second look will often catch errors you missed.

An effective functional qualifications brief is a real challenge to compose. Take the time to assess an employer's needs, evaluate your assets, and target specific goals. Someone who just wants a job need not write a qualifications brief. However, if you desire to start with a career that best uses your abilities and experience, with room for growth, your time and effort will be well worth it.

Review the following practical points for composing your qualifications brief:

- Your qualifications brief should reflect your character and personality. Do not adapt someone else's qualifications brief to fit your own experiences or have anyone else prepare it. An ability to "sell" yourself is essential, and to do so in person, you must first be able to get the facts down on paper.

- State your career objective based on what you want to do and where you want to do it. It should be stated in terms of your abilities and accomplishments supported by your education and experience to date.

- Arrange the sections of your brief in a way that emphasizes your strong points and supports your career objective. Place your most qualifying strength, experience, ability, or accomplishment first, followed by your next most qualifying, and so on.

- Emphasize your abilities, qualifications, and accomplishments more than duties and responsibilities.

- Cite specific examples of your successes and accomplishments.

- Be concise. Use simple, direct language. When describing your strengths, keep descriptions in concise paragraphs or individual sentences with bullets.

- Use the active voice; use action verbs such as conducted, saved, managed, achieved, evaluated, compiled, and improvised.

- Proofread and have someone else proofread your final typed copy for errors, and ask for comments on presentation.

Qualifications brief worksheet

Job experience. In the spaces provided below, list each job you have held since high school. These should include internships and volunteer work. Write down the title of each job or a specific description of the job, the name of the company or organization you worked for, and the dates you worked there. For example, possible entries might read

1. Research Assistant, Seattle Park District, 1983-84
or
2. Sports and Crafts initiator, Seattle Handicapped Citizens Center, 1982-83

After listing each job, answer each subsequent question. Try to remember everything you can about each position. Some of your answers will be straightforward; others will require more thought.

Job title　Company　Dates of employment

1. _____

2. _____

3. _____

4. _____

5. _____

The following questions should be answered for each job listed above (the numbers should correspond). If additional space is needed for your answer or if you have listed more than 5 jobs, attach a separate sheet of paper. Try to be as specific as possible with your answers, but include everything. In this way, all the information can be easily reviewed if and when you rewrite your qualifications brief. Make additions to this list whenever you can.

- What specific activities did you perform in a typical week?

  1. _____

  2. _____

  3. _____

  4. _____

  5. _____

- What activities did you perform in any special assignments or projects you worked on (e.g., developing surveys, coaching sports, teaching crafts)?

  1. _____
  2. _____
  3. _____
  4. _____
  5. _____

- What skills and abilities did you use in these daily, weekly, or special activities (e.g., conducting evaluations, initiating activities to enhance interest, teaching, coaching)?

  1. _____
  2. _____
  3. _____
  4. _____
  5. _____

- What were your accomplishments? What changes, if any, were made as a result of your work (e.g., increased participation in activities, demand for more activities, new programs to encourage self-sufficiency)?

  1. _____
  2. _____
  3. _____
  4. _____
  5. _____

- What new skills and abilities did you acquire as a result of this job?

  1. _____
  2. _____
  3. _____
  4. _____
  5. _____

- What did you enjoy most?

  1. _____
  2. _____
  3. _____
  4. _____
  5. _____

- What were your personal, social, or material (salary, benefits) rewards in this position?

  1. _____
  2. _____
  3. _____
  4. _____
  5. _____

- What was your reason for leaving?

  1. _____
  2. _____
  3. _____
  4. _____
  5. _____

Education.

- What psychology degrees have you earned, or are you going to earn, and in what particular area or areas?

  _____
  _____
  _____

- What was the general theme of the psychology courses you selected to take (e.g., developmental, social, experimental)?

  _____
  _____
  _____
  _____

- What electives did you take?

_____

_____

_____

_____

_____

- What special honors, awards, or scholarships did you receive?

_____

_____

_____

_____

- What courses did you most enjoy? Why?

_____

_____

_____

_____

_____

_____

- What extracurricular activities did you participate in? What special skills did you acquire through them?

_____

_____

_____

_____

_____

- What professional organizations or societies did you join?

_____

_____

_____

Personal experience. List all the situations and skills not connected with employment or school that you feel might be relevant to a prospective employer. For instance, as the result of a previous job, what, if anything, did you learn about organizing people? Time? Materials? What did you learn about communicating with supervisors? Peers?

_____

_____

_____

_____

PART 5

Beyond the bachelor's degree

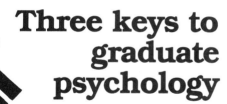

Three keys to graduate psychology

T his chapter focuses on the strategies that must be applied by those undergraduate psychology majors seeking to get into graduate programs in psychology. It may be surprising that those planning to enter graduate school make up only a small proportion of psychology graduates. Why, then, should there be any need for strategies to get advanced degrees?

Remembering the fairly uncomplicated transition from high school to college, many students think that a similar transition takes place between undergraduate and graduate study. Not so! The competition for graduate school acceptance in psychology is keen. At some schools the acceptance rate is less than 2%. The competition is similar to that for medical school. However, if you truly want to continue in psychology, are willing to take the time needed for preparation, and develop a reasonable application strategy, you will probably be accepted in a graduate program, although not necessarily at your first- or even second-choice school.

Job opportunities in traditional settings, such as in colleges, hospitals, and clinics, are gradually declining. One exception is state and local governments, in which opportunities are increasing. There is a good job market for psychologists, but it's a different market: PhDs will now have to seek new and emerging careers in which their training and expertise can be fully utilized (for further information on new and emerging careers see chapter 11 of this book; see also *Careers in Psychology*, APA, 1986).

The decision to attend graduate school in psychology, therefore, should really be because you desire to become a psychologist. You should ask yourself where becoming a psychologist falls in your list of priorities. If you have other goals or obligations that have a higher priority, these may limit your chances of getting into graduate school. For example, if you

Material for this chapter was contributed by Patricia W. Lunneborg, University of Washington, and Vicki M. Wilson, Hospital Commission, Olympia, WA.

decide to remain in your home town, such a decision limits your chances for advanced study. To maximize your chances of getting in, you must apply to schools at various locations. The fact is that not everyone who would like to go on in psychology wants it more than anything else in life. There may be other things that are more important to you. However, the fewer restrictions you put on becoming a psychologist (I must live here, I must attend school there), the greater the chances are that you will make it.

After considering where becoming a psychologist falls in your list of priorities, you might look at alternative ways of meeting your career goals and discover that graduate school in psychology might not be right for you after all. You might find that a program in social work, educational psychology, business, public affairs, guidance and counseling, law, nutrition, occupational therapy, special education, and so forth, might be more appropriate to your needs and desires and less difficult to enter. Throughout this book you will find information to help you explore various opportunities in these and other directions.

If you do decide to continue in psychology, what should you do? There are three keys to getting into a graduate program in psychology: *persistence*, *preparation*, and *application know-how*.

Persistence

Webster's defines persistence as "stubborn or enduring continuance, as in a chosen course or purpose." Essentially, it means hanging in there until you make it. No matter what obstacles appear and regardless of whatever pessimistic advice you receive, you must maintain dedication to your academic goals and career objectives and refuse to be deterred. Graduate schools look favorably on those who demonstrate decisiveness. One student, against her faculty's advice, decided that there was only one graduate school for her. After applying there for three consecutive years she was finally accepted. Each time she was rejected, however, she found out the reason for the rejection and worked to correct the deficiency. Her dedication and willingness to work hard finally paid off.

Preparation

Preparation in this context means using your undergraduate years to acquire attractive credentials. As a potential graduate student, you will be judged on a number of criteria that vary in importance depending on the orientation of individual graduate school depart-

ments. These criteria include cumulative grade point average (GPA), psychology GPA, scores on the Graduate Record Examination (GRE) and Miller Analogies Test (MAT), general academic coursework, science background, research experience, letters of recommendation, and clinical experience. If a graduate department, for instance, is strong in research and is heavily funded by grants, it may favor candidates with strong science, laboratory, statistics, and research backgrounds. Since large, traditional programs are research oriented, they tend to look for candidates with similar backgrounds. If you are interested in clinical or counseling psychology, research is important, but field experience is also necessary. It is critical to be able to offer graduate program administrators proof that you have tried the field of clinical or counseling psychology and know what is involved. In short, if you are a student willing to take the time to accumulate a solid background in the hard sciences, such as math, biology, or chemistry, and include in your psychology major laboratories, statistics, research, and fieldwork, if appropriate, you may be well on the road to acceptance by a graduate program.

Academic background. Once students know what is needed, they usually want to know how much is needed. There is no one right answer. How much of any one element needed to make you attractive as a candidate for a graduate program depends on the emphasis of individual graduate departments. A general rule is that a minimum of 10 quarter credits each of math, physical sciences, and biological sciences is necessary. Add to this one year of clinical work, if appropriate. Combining all of these courses with desired electives, you can see why your undergraduate career may stretch to 5 years, particularly if your decision to go to graduate school is not made early in your college career.

The best approach, therefore, is a conservative one—excellent preparation in all areas. Of course, there are always exceptions to the rules, both by students and program administrators. For instance, one student accepted as a psychology graduate student did not major in psychology as an undergraduate, another refused to get involved in research, and another had a science background consisting only of oceanography. These students are to be congratulated for their successes, but not modeled. Individual programs can also be unusual. Although this chapter concerns preparation for the typical traditional graduate program in psychology, there are humanistic and clinical programs that place less emphasis on science and research as undergraduate requirements.

Research and fieldwork. Research experience for you as an undergraduate can be obtained by linking up with faculty in your department and working as a research assistant. Eventually, you may progress to doing your own research and possibly even co-author some publications; graduate schools are extremely impressed by that. Some institutions have undergraduate research or independent study courses that make obtaining research experience that much easier. However, it is not the accumulation of credits that is important. What is important for you is to have done research over an extended period of time and to have developed a close professional relationship with faculty members.

If you need clinical field experience but your school has no practicum programs, simply open the Yellow Pages, find local mental health agencies, hospitals, or other agencies of interest, and volunteer to help. You should make clear to the agency the type of experience you desire—counseling, interviewing, testing, research—and keep looking until you find it. This process is much easier than it sounds, since most mental health agencies are half-staffed by volunteers.

Letters of recommendation. You cannot expect to come up with three strong letters of recommendation without having cultivated a few sources. For students attending small colleges where the normal class size is less than 30, finding faculty sources is usually not a problem. However, for those attending a university where courses can have as many as 200 students, getting to know faculty becomes a real challenge. In such universities, faculty members you may have worked with on research are the best sources of letters. These professors are able to evaluate you in terms of research ability, critical scholarship, written communication, professional identification, emotional stability, effective energy, and interpersonal relations. They can also provide an overall judgment of the likelihood of your success. For clinical or counseling students, fieldwork supervisors are another excellent source for letters of recommendation.

What kinds of letters should you have? In general, you should have at least three solid academic references. For clinical or counseling students, two academic references and one fieldwork reference are impressive. Some schools are now asking for four letters, so be prepared. However, as a courtesy to those reviewing your application, do not overkill by sending more than five letters.

Graduate Record Examination and Miller Analogies Test. The finale in your preparation is taking the GRE and, possibly, the MAT. The

GRE consists of two separate tests, the General Test and Subject Test in psychology. The General Test is required by essentially every graduate program in psychology and contains three sections measuring verbal, quantitative, and analytical abilities, resulting in three scores. The Subject Test, which is not required by all programs, is designed to measure knowledge and understanding of psychological principles and facts basic to advanced study, providing an overall score as well as experimental and social subscores. The verbal and quantitative scores are commonly viewed as most important. To determine whether a school requires both the General and Subject Tests, consult *Graduate Study in Psychology* (APA, 1986) revised annually. (This book is available in bookstores or can be ordered directly from APA with the order blank appearing in this volume.)

The GRE is administered five times each year with test dates in October, December, February, April, and June (General Test only). The General Test is given in the morning and the Subject Test in the afternoon. The admissions office, testing office, or Career Counseling Center at your college or university should have copies of the most recent *GRE Information Bulletin* (including the test application form and sample questions), published by the Educational Testing Service. Or you can obtain a copy by writing to Graduate Record Examination, CN 6000, Princeton, NJ 08541-6000.

Should you study for the GRE? Yes! Studying is critical. There are two basic purposes for studying for the GREs: to increase speed and to reduce anxiety. Reviewing will bring to mind material you once learned but have not recently used. Becoming familiar with the nature of the material beforehand will also speed you in taking the test and reduce the anxiety you may feel upon entering the examination room. A GRE study guide, widely available at bookstores, can assist you in preparing for the verbal and quantitative sections of the General Test. For the Subject Test in Psychology, reviewing as many current introductory psychology texts as possible is the best study method.

What about timing? The GRE should be taken in October of your senior year of undergraduate study or the October preceding the year in which you would like to start graduate school. Some program application deadlines are as early as December, and most cluster around January and early February for admission the following fall semester. Completing the test in October leaves ample time for distributing test scores and for solving any problems that may arise.

How important is the GRE? Very important. But remember, it is only one of several criteria that will be evaluated. You should acknowledge the GRE's importance, study hard for it, do as well as possible, and then follow through with an application strategy that is appropriate for your test scores. For example, poorer-than-average test scores may mean narrowing your list of prospective graduate programs. Furthermore, you should consider the GRE as a one-time endeavor. Even though the test can be retaken, the Educational Testing Service reports *all* scores, and the first scores are generally regarded as the most valid. There is also a 50-50 chance of your getting a poorer second score. Most students do not do significantly better on a second try.

The MAT, on the other hand, is required by about 25% of all graduate programs. The test consists of 100 analogies arranged in order of increasing complexity. Scores range from 0 to 100, and the time limit is 50 minutes. The MAT is distributed by the Psychological Corporation, which publishes a valuable booklet that describes the test and application procedures and lists testing centers and 60 practice analogies. The booklet can be obtained free of charge from the Psychological Corporation, 304 East 85th Street, New York, NY 10017. Since the MAT is required from about 25% of all graduate programs, find out whether it is required from those programs you are interested in. However, if you have yet to decide what schools to apply to, you may want to schedule to take the MAT anyway.

Application schedule. A suggested schedule for your undergraduate years is provided for you in this chapter (Scott & Davis-Silka, 1974). This schedule represents an ideal. Unless your decision to attend graduate school is made during the first year of college, you will not be able to follow the schedule exactly. For example, if your decision to major in psychology is not made until your junior year, it is next to impossible for you to build attractive credentials in one year. With imagination, however, you can adapt the schedule to your plans. Students applying to graduate school for the fall, when the majority of programs accept students, should apply almost a year ahead of the anticipated admission time. Your most impressive coursework must be completed by approximately December of your senior year. This does not apply to those delaying graduate study. Those students will be able to submit their entire records.

Résumé and letter of intent. The résumé and the letter of intent, both mentioned in the suggested schedule, should be sent to prospective schools. The résumé outlines your educational background, work and field experience, and research (see chapters 13 and 14 for advice on writing résumés and qualifications briefs). The letter of intent is a description of (a) the development of your academic interests, (b) research experience, (c) clinical or counseling interests and experience, (d) unique abilities and skills relevant to psychology (e.g., computer programming), (e) graduate goals, (f) reasons for wanting to attend a particular graduate school, and (g) professional goals. The letter should not be a complete autobiography; if a particular psychology program wants other information, this will be specified in the application materials.

The letter of intent has some standard parts and some that are specific to particular programs. As an applicant, you should be aware that even as a qualified individual, you will probably not be accepted into a program whose specific emphasis is not clearly reflected in your application materials. You must be very sure of your direction and area of specialization, and build the letters of intent around them. The goals stated must be compatible with the prospective program.

Suggested Schedule For Career Planning and Applying to Graduate School

Sophomore Year

- After completing most of the general education requirements in your first year of college, work on the basic psychology requirements, including statistics, laboratory, and science courses.

- Become acquainted with several faculty members in the psychology department, who may be able to write letters of recommendation for you later.

- Write a preliminary résumé.

- Attend departmental colloquiums.

Junior Year

- Continue, and try to complete, basic requirements.

- Begin research with faculty and continue throughout junior year.

- Begin to consider letter-of-recommendation resources (e.g., research supervisors, and professors of small classes).

- Explore opportunities for joining professional organizations (e.g., obtain faculty sponsorship for a student membership in the American Psychological Association).

- Redraft preliminary résumé.

- Attend the state's annual psychological meeting.

- Do fieldwork if interested in clinical or counseling psychology.

- Begin work on a paper on your previous research for possible publication or presentation. (Start in spring of junior year.)

Summer Between Junior and Senior Years

- Buy study guides for the GRE and MAT and begin studying.

- Begin to investigate prospective graduate programs (consult with faculty and use library resources).

- Write a third draft of your résumé.

- From research work, write papers for publication or presentation.

Senior Year

- Complete all impressive degree requirements, research, and fieldwork by December. Continue the research and fieldwork, however, because they may be helpful later on.

- September: (a) Buy the current issue of *Graduate Study in Psychology* and write to prospective schools for application materials; (b) register in September to take the October GRE; and (c) begin requesting letters of recommendation.

- Through application materials, find out about any additional requirements or tests needed by individual graduate school programs.

- November: (a) Have letter of intent written and a polished résumé completed and (b) have a faculty member or adviser check them for grammar, spelling, and content.

- December: (a) Send completed applications to schools way ahead of deadlines; (b) request transcripts to be sent from all colleges attended; and (c) if you are not going on to graduate school immediately, continue research, fieldwork, and faculty affiliations as long as possible.

Application know-how

The third key to getting into graduate school is knowing the mechanics of applying—where to get information on prospective programs, how many programs to select, strategy in selection, financial aid, and timing. Four excellent sources of information are available. First, and most comprehensive, is *Graduate Study in Psychology*, which provides general advice on applying and specific information (including departments and addresses, programs and degrees offered, application procedures, admission requirements, tuition, and financial assistance) for hundreds of graduate programs in psychology in the United States and Canada. This book is a must!

Another must book to read, is *Preparing for Graduate Study: Not for Seniors Only!* (Fretz & Stang, 1983). This 90-page booklet supplements and exceeds the material covered in this chapter and in fact should be utilized as fully by everyone considering graduate study in psychology. It provides detailed information on degrees, undergraduate preparation, application procedures, financial aid, and success in graduate school. Written in a clear and understandable style, the booklet is lightweight and inexpensive. Get this book right away! (Order forms for *Grad Study* and *Not for Seniors Only* are supplied in this book.)

A third good source of application information is the psychology department faculty. Professors aware of your interests and abilities can use their knowledge of various programs to advise you on the most appropriate schools to apply to. And a fourth source is the library. By going through relevant journals, you can find out who is writing articles that interest you and which schools these authors are affiliated with.

The result of this research should be a list of from 20 to 30 prospective graduate schools and programs. If your college or university has catalogs from other colleges, look through these to consider programs in order to eliminate some from your list immediately. For those programs remaining, a typed postcard should be sent to the chairperson of each program requesting information on the program, a catalog, and application and financial aid forms. You can then use this information to trim the list down to the finalists.

How many schools and what type of school should be on that final list? The list should consist of not less than 10 schools that represent a range in quality, geographic location, and level of degree offered. There are two main reasons for this type of distribution: The competition you face with other applicants and the limited control you have over the selection process.

Even though as an applicant you can exercise some control over graduate school acceptance, there are some aspects of the process that you cannot control. For example, you may be rejected by a school that at the last minute decides not to take anyone from a particular geographic area. The rejection is not because you are an unattractive candidate but because the school's department simply has made this sort of decision. Or subjective criteria may enter in: objective criteria, including GRE scores, cumulative and psychology GPAs, and science background, are sometimes weighed according to a graduate department's orientation and combined to predict the success of each applicant. Once a final group of top candidates is chosen, it is often difficult to choose from among them. A selection committee might choose a candidate who impressed them by making the trip to the department to be interviewed, for example.

Another reason for applying to a wide range of schools is simply the problem of interpreting admissions criteria. In *Graduate Study in Psychology*, schools rate non-objective criteria like letters of recommendation and work experience as high, medium, or low in importance. Each department knows precisely what these ratings mean, but how can an applicant know? How high is high? Even with objective admissions criteria, there can be a huge difference between meeting stated minimum requirements and being competitive. To allow a margin of safety for what cannot be controlled, no matter how excellent a candidate you are, you should apply to at least 10 programs.

Doctoral programs are harder to get into than master's programs. All students should apply to some master's-only programs. "Master's only" refers to schools that specialize in master's programs and do not offer a PhD. (Generally, if a school reports that it grants both MA and PhD degrees, it means that it is really in the business of producing PhDs.) As a guideline for choosing the 10 schools to apply to, you might want to include 3 or 4 PhD programs you truly would like to attend, another 4 or 5 PhD programs you would not mind attending, and 2 or 3 master's-only programs.

You might be confused by this application strategy because you have probably been told that if you cannot attend a prestigious institution, you might as well not go to graduate school. Or you may wonder about applying to master's-only programs when you really want to apply to PhD programs. It would be great to be accepted by one of the top schools in the country; however, there are only so many top programs and they fill only so many slots. In considering schools further down your list, you should remember that you decided to continue in psychology because you believe psychology is the area in which you really want an education and therefore are willing to get that education anywhere possible.

Master's programs are another excellent way to work toward a PhD. They are less difficult to enter and, if your undergraduate career has been less than glowing, may be just the ticket to that PhD. After completing your MA, you can then apply to PhD programs with a better chance of entering the school you want, since more emphasis will be placed on your graduate-level work rather than your undergraduate career.

What about costs, and how much time will you need? Probably $300 to $400 minimum, depending on the number of schools you apply to. The average application fee is $25. Add to that the cost of official transcripts (from every college you attended), duplication costs for recommendations, résumés, and letters of intent, postage, and even long-distance phone calls. Also, the amount of time you spend on a difficult, 5-credit course. Hundreds of hours are needed for the application process, so plan your course schedule accordingly.

However, remember this important point: If you need financial assistance while in graduate school, apply for it! Routinely ask for financial aid forms along with the graduate school applications when you write. Graduate school is a full-time job that will not leave time for much else. Programs with a tradition of supplying financial aid are still providing it. Stating that you do not need financial assistance will not necessarily help you get accepted, unless the reason is that you have a scholarship or similar funding.

Finally, get started early. Keep in mind that it will be necessary to apply to programs a year before entering. Begin to meet faculty early in your undergraduate career, complete the most impressive coursework, such as statistics, as soon as possible, start selecting prospective programs early (not two weeks before deadlines), and allow for procrastination on the part of professors preparing your letters of recommendation. Definitely follow up on such requests.

If you do not continue your graduate education right away, everything mentioned in this chapter still applies. Most important, by the end of your undergraduate career, you should have letters of recommendation and your test scores on file. If you remain out of school for an extended period, the original recommendations will be there for you to use. In addition, even if you are not planning to go the graduate school immediately, take the GRE and MAT while you are still an undergraduate or within a few months of graduation. Students out of school for any extended period get out of the habit of taking exams and their exam-taking ability decreases. GRE and MAT scores remain valid for 5 years, so if you are delaying your graduate education, plan accordingly.

There is no evidence that not going on to graduate school immediately is detrimental to your chances of acceptance. Factors that indicate a higher level of maturity—employment, postbaccalaureate studies, years of research, and clinical experience—are gaining significance in the selection process. However, it would be detrimental to disconnect yourself from the study or world or psychology. Always keep a foot in the door as an indication of commitment to the field. If you can't find employment in a psychology-related field right away, at least do volunteer research or related fieldwork. The stronger your continued commitment to psychology, the greater your chance of future acceptance into graduate school.

Here are some reminders for success:

1. Start the application process early (no later than the summer before the fall you apply). It takes time to write a résumé and letters of intent. You might want to take a lighter course load the fall quarter you apply.

2. If you blow the GREs, spend your time on the areas in which you have better control. Get good grades and do lots of research as best you can. Impress faculty with your reliability and creativity so they will write good letters of recommendation.

3. Choose prospective schools based on the match between their training goals and your professional goals. Success and pleasure in graduate education come only from a good match.

4. A positive attitude is important. It shows in your applications, letters, and résumé. Don't apply to graduate school until you are ready. Then confidently go for it!

References

Fretz, B.R., & Stang, D.J. (1980). *Preparing for graduate study in psychology: Not for seniors only!* Washington, DC: American Psychological Association.

Scott, W.C., & Davis-Silka, L. (1974). Applying to graduate school in psychology: A perspective and guide. *JSAS Catalog of Selected Documents in Psychology, 4,* 33 (Ms. No. 597).

Chapter 16

A survival manual
for new hires

What to expect
in the workplace

A significant number of recent liberal arts college graduates are having trouble adjusting to the technical needs and cultural requirements of the workplace. Their problems stem from a lack of technical skills and unrealistic job expectations to barriers put up by employers and co-workers who seem unwilling to accept new hires without business backgrounds. This chapter pertains to the socialization process that most new hires face on entering the workplace and offers the psychology major helpful pointers on how to cope with this transition period and adapt to the new employment experience. As a new employee, you must understand the structure of the workplace, with its role requirements and rules for job performance (Allaire & Firsirotu, 1985). You will probably be expected to be accountable for your performance according to specific plans and timetables provided by your supervisors, which are not usually flexible. As a new hire, you will likely be subjected to periodic formal and informal evaluations in order to shape your behavior to fit the company's design and plan of the particular position for which you have been employed. Since evaluations should serve as constructive feedback on your progress, do not be discouraged if you and your work are frequently critiqued. Try to learn quickly and improve on the job you have as best you can. The better your development on the job, the sooner your supervisors will trust and value you as an employee.

Occasionally, however, new hires find themselves in a high-pressure or hostile workplace, caused by either poor selection or placement procedures, bad management, or unsympathetic co-workers. Sometimes high-pressure environments are consciously constructed by companies in the belief that competition

Material for this chapter was contributed by Judith Waters, Fairleigh Dickinson University; Justina Ayers, AT&T Communications; and Benjamin Drew, Fairleigh Dickinson University. The contributors to this chapter wish to thank M. Michael Cutler of AT&T Communications for his astute observations on the problems of new hires and for his editorial expertise.

makes workers more productive. Although some people work well in such situations, others do not. If you find yourself in a stressful work environment, make the most of what you have, but don't give up! See whether you can adapt or, after some time, look for an alternative position.

Perceptions held by employers. In a recent survey of 30 employment agency placement counselors and corporate management career development executives in the New York metropolitan area, respondents were asked to list the assets and liabilities they felt that college graduates brought to their first jobs. Of the assets, they listed the following traits as common among recent graduates:

- enthusiasm
- drive
- curiosity
- an eagerness to learn
- open-mindedness
- flexibility
- adaptability.

Among the liabilities were the following:

- an inability to set priorities
- an inability to distinguish formal from informal systems within the organization
- an inability to confront problems quickly
- immature conduct
- an inability to adjust quickly to a 9-to-5 schedule
- unrealistic expectations concerning promotions
- a know-it-all attitude
- a lack of interpersonal skills.

A major concern expressed by almost all the respondents centers on the college graduate's lack of real work experience and need for considerable on-the-job training. They felt that 6 months to a year were needed before a new employee was fully integrated into an organization. Although all new hires need some sort of on-the-job training, such a liability can be overcome by showing a willingness to learn and an eagerness to participate fully. Respondents also expressed concern about the perception in the business world that psychology majors examine anything and everything that people say and do, looking for hidden meanings. (Be careful not to practice psychology without a license.) Some respondents observed that recent graduates also lack interpersonal skills especially when dealing with less-educated co-workers. Other employers view liberal arts majors as having a humanistic orientation that is at odds with the profit-oriented

goals of business. The idea of cost-effectiveness is applied to most organizational decisions. Although not every employer will have these concerns, new hires must be aware of the potential problems such views pose.

As you have read throughout this book, your personal characteristics play a much more important role in your being selected for a job than does your specific college major. Many employers look for individuals with potential regardless of degree. Moreover, some employers find it difficult to distinguish between a psychology degree and any other liberal arts degree. However, if you point out that as a psychology major you have taken courses in statistics and computer-related subjects, have done research, and have written reports, the employer will be more impressed with the relevance of your skills to the organization. By showing an employer functional aspects of your learning, you allow the employer to better evaluate your potential to the organization in terms that he or she can understand.

The enculturation process. Every business, profession, or industry has its own ways of doing things that involve an understanding of behavior, values, and traditions associated with that particular organization. These elements constitute the culture of the workplace. The process of learning that culture is called socialization or enculturation. Organizations have many methods of socializing workers besides formal training. In the past, for example, the history and stories of a company contained important information about "how things get done around here." Today, many companies have formal and informal orientation programs to help new hires adjust to their new environment.

Social control in business is achieved through a system of rewards and punishments expressed by promotion and monetary incen-

tives. The new hire is expected to respond to even the most subtle aspects of the corporate culture because his or her job depends on an understanding of and skill in using the organization. The new hire must, however, be able to distinguish the differences between formal titles and actual functional relationships. Any change in management personnel will also affect both formal and informal relationships since leadership styles differ. The behavior one supervisor respects, another may find ineffective or even offensive.

The process of enculturation in each organization reflects its unique social environment and standard operating procedures. Part of the process includes the do's and don'ts of "how things get done around here." Some typical "around here-isms" you may encounter include the following:

- We don't put in extra effort unless we get paid for it.

- We don't get paid for overtime, it's expected of us.

- We don't work too hard and make our co-workers look bad.

- We look to the unofficial leaders, not the official supervisors, for direction.

- We don't think for ourselves, we do as we are told.

Knowing the informal rules will save you time and trouble. You must always exercise discretion in choosing between formal rules and around here-isms.

How to ensure your success in the workplace

The following are some points for you to consider for success in the workplace. This advice can play a helpful role in your transition from the world of study to the world of work.

Acquiring business-related education and knowledge. Students who have not taken business courses may be unfamiliar with some of the standard operating procedures of businesses. They may even be perceived by potential employers as having no real commitment to a career in business, or as being arrogant and holding condescending attitudes toward the business community. Employers probably resent the idea that liberal arts applicants think they can get jobs in the business world without some formal preparation.

To counteract this attitude, you may want to familiarize yourself with business activity by taking business courses while in college, reading books and periodicals on business, or

working for a time in a business environment. Participating in a work-study or internship program with a business is the best way to show potential employers your desire to work. Remember to highlight such work experience on your resume or in conversation with an employer when you begin to seek employment. In addition, you should be aware of the vocabulary of business so that you can communicate effectively on the job.

Having realistic job expectations. Many liberal arts graduates expect that once hired they will master the necessary job skills quickly and be promoted rapidly. Some expect high salaries within a short time, quick entry into career development programs, and meaningful input into policy-making decisions. Don't deceive yourself! In reality, as a new hire, you can anticipate a humbling beginning, designed to make you conform to the demands of the company. Management will usually expect you to be almost invisible, to do what you are told, and to respond immediately to feedback on your performance.

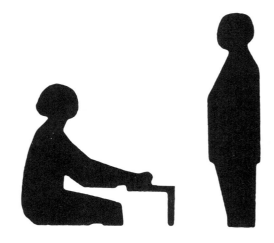

Although this sounds threatening, don't be discouraged. Remember that you are new to the job, and until you have acquired significant experience, don't expect instant advancement, independence, or any significant responsibility. You may want to downplay your immediate expectations and concentrate on the task at hand.

Understanding your job description. Unless your job description is presented clearly, you may, in fact, have less of an idea about what is expected of you as a new hire than you had as a student. When you were an undergraduate, you knew approximately what kind of work would be necessary to achieve a particular grade in each course. In the business world, task requirements may be ambiguous.

As a new hire, don't feel insecure if your job lacks specific guidelines by which you can determine your task requirements and understand the limits of your responsibility. In smaller organizations, conditions may require that roles overlap and that workers develop many skills with no established boundaries between jobs. Although such ambiguities can be disturbing, they can also provide opportunities for growth. As a new hire, you should approach them as challenges to test your personal management of time and ability to organize. You should be able to learn all facets of the business and become adept in dealing with co-workers, clients, and supervisors.

Orienting yourself to the workplace. Even if your company has a formal orientation program, it cannot present all the information necessary for good job performance. Moreover, the informal and widely accepted practices and working relationships may even be in direct conflict with the formal procedures and hierarchy as presented in the orientation program. There are also informal practices and networks that are never to be openly discussed, even among friendly co-workers. You may be left to discover on your own who has the real authority. You must become an effective problem solver, learning how to get the information you need and how to utilize that information to your advantage.

An orientation program does assist the new hire in becoming acclimated to organizational environments. Few employees, however, are ever exposed to such programs since more than 80% will work for companies that are too small to afford the expense involved or that see little justification in making the effort. These organizations still expect new hires to demonstrate their potential quickly or be replaced.

There is no doubt that getting the job is sometimes easier than keeping the job! Today, in a labor market with many more qualified applicants than there are positions available, it is critical to possess or develop the skills necessary to become a valued employee in a short time. Recent graduates are relatively untried commodities for the business world. The consensus is that new hires must start at the bottom and demonstrate their worth to the company. The specific tasks may not even be important. Organizations often cannot or will not risk their resources on inexperienced individuals. New hires, on the other hand, are looking for exciting work and challenging opportunities to display their skills, whereas the organization is doing everything it can to prevent being negatively affected by the mistakes of novices. What the organization does expect

from you as a new hire is the ability to assimilate and synthesize information and to apply that knowledge to limited practical issues in problem-solving situations. It's very much like doing homework.

Developing good communication skills. Good communication skills, verbal and written, include (a) the ability to listen, (b) the ability to respond to feedback, (c) the ability to solve or analyze problems, and (d) interpersonal skills. The development of listening skills is extremely important. The successful completion of a task is often hampered by the fact that many individuals stop listening before they fully understand what is required of them.

Sometimes, they have preconceived notions about how the job should be done. As a new hire, you must listen carefully to what is being said and then ask for clarification if you are unsure of the instructions.

Relatively few new hires on the entry level are asked to analyze serious problem situations and make recommendations that will have a significant impact on the organization. However, you should be aware of the similarities and differences in problem-solving processes between your typical experiences with research in school and the conditions under which reports are formulated in business. In business, this process is performed under a tight schedule and is often based on limited information rather than on exhaustive research. Moreover, the implementation of recommendations may have an immediate impact on the organization. The business community usually has a need for quick, incisive approaches to problems, in contrast to the slow, deliberate, analytic style of academia. Expediency and cost-effectiveness are the basis for business problem solving.

You may often be called upon to communicate in writing. Reports written in business and industry are generally short, sometimes composed in outline form, and come directly to the point without an elaborate introduction. Most executives would like to have the problem identified, any critical issues outlined, and the preferred solution described on one or two pages at most. Brevity appears to be the order of the day.

Interpersonal skills are particularly important for new hires. Interpersonal relationships in university settings are somewhat unique to the academic world and may, in fact, prove to be an impediment in making a successful transition to business. As a student, you relate mainly to peers, faculty, and office staff, having personal contact with members of the administration only when there are problems. These relationships do not involve the daily scrutiny of activities that the new hire experiences in the workplace. If you are not used to constant supervision by an authority figure, you may find yourself suffering from evaluation apprehension. If this occurs, try to learn some stress management techniques to help you cope.

Managing time effectively. As a new hire, you are no longer on an academic calendar. You no longer have winter and spring breaks or a long summer vacation. You no longer have the freedom you once had to arrange your own schedule of classes and activities based on course offerings and availability; to plan your own free time; to talk, eat, or socialize when you wish; or to delay or be excused from papers or exams. The rules governing workplace performance and scheduling are quite different. Depending on the particular job, most employees are expected to conform to a regular time schedule—5 days a week, 8 hours a day. New hires do not usually have the flexibility to plan their own work schedules. Meeting deadlines is critical. Excuses are usually not tolerated. And there are fewer and shorter vacations as well as less time for social activity.

Efficient time management is one of the major requirements for any employee. Supervisors and managers usually assign specific schedules for job performance, the operation of the department, or for meeting deadlines. Conflicts and problems do arise; therefore, as a new employee, be prepared to adjust. By an-

ticipating delays and developing contingency plans for emergencies, you will be under less pressure, and of greater value to the organization. Being on-time for meetings is critical. Always plan to be early. As a rule, consider the worst case scenario in advance and take the necessary steps to avoid it.

Working as a team. Unlike college, where you are taught to think critically and independently and where original ideas are encouraged to be pursued, the business world emphasizes teamwork and cooperation. New hires are expected to conform to the norms of the organization and make fewer independent decisions. Your organization's emphasis on teamwork and cooperation promotes the performance of the department at the sake of individual creativity. The trick for you is to be smart enough to know when teamwork is a priority and when individual initiative is valued.

Appreciating the profit motive. There is a common perception among business people that liberal arts majors fresh out of college disdain the profit motive, preferring instead to concentrate on loftier abstract ideals. Liberal arts majors are seen as being unable to act quickly on decisions, unable to balance costs and benefits, and as being financially irresponsible. Although these perceptions may not apply to you, you will have to demonstrate that your head is not in the clouds. And remember the practical objectives and goals of your job position. Budgetary considerations are of utmost importance in the professional world.

Using the performance evaluation to your advantage. New hires have to be in the proper frame of mind to benefit from their performance evaluations. Many people do not deal with criticism well. They are defensive. They spend time preparing counterarguments instead of listening to the content of the evaluation. Feedback may be formal (a written report or a performance appraisal interview) or informal. It can be a positive response to a job well done or it can also be a gentle (or not so gentle) warning that improvement is needed. You must be attentive to how your work is being evaluated. Constant behavior modification is necessary for success on the job.

In order to function effectively in a job, new hires must assess not only the mistakes that are being made, but also any "sins of omission." They must question whether or not they are doing everything they can or should be doing. There may also be times when a defense or an explanation of your actions actually is in order. Any explanation will be better received if it focuses on the issues without irrelevant digressions. Spontaneous but ill-conceived responses to criticism only create more problems, so deferring an explanation to a calmer moment may be the wisest course of action.

Students have survived many years of formal education by doing their homework. Being prepared on the job is not so different from being prepared for class. As a new hire, you will always be in need of quick study skills. Sometimes the enculturation process, in the form of the orientation program, the job description, or supervisor training, does not provide all the information needed for good job performance. In that case, you should seek advice either from veteran employees, other supervisory personnel, informal networks, business-oriented publications, or professional organizations. You can also take graduate-level courses.

Understanding office politics. Your awareness and understanding of office politics is critical to your success in the business world. A supervisor, for example, may feel threatened by your zeal to impress others and prove yourself. You may unintentionally oversell the value of your education. Your supervisor, in turn, may overemphasize the value of work experience and ignore your best ideas. Just remember who's the boss!

Another important problem of office politics is the issue of maintaining confidentiality. Social conversations outside the workplace can easily turn to your job. The most casual remark can have serious consequences. Be careful not to spread rumors. Even if you are sure of your facts, it's best to be careful about what you say concerning your office. Don't feel compelled to impress friends about what you know. Be professional when discussing professional matters.

Dressing appropriately. On most college campuses, students are relatively free to dress the way they choose. Businesses, however, may have formal or unwritten dress codes. In addition, specific occupations and organizations have personal images that are projected by their employees. Bankers, for example, maintain a very conservative appearance. The field of advertising generally encourages a more avant-garde look. In any event, a reasonable guideline is to select clothing that is not intrusive. What a person wears or how his or her hair looks should never be more important or more interesting than what that person has to say. You should dress to appear competent and avoid ostentatious display.

If you are really serious about being accepted on the job, some degree of conformity will be expected. Try to maintain good grooming habits and a professional look. Many people buy a suitable outfit for interviewing, but once hired mistakenly feel that they no longer have to be concerned about making a good impression. Most companies expect their employees to present a professional appearance at all times.

Manners. Formal manners and polite speech are expected in almost every organization. Recent college graduates may not be familiar with some of the rules. New hires, for example, may not be aware of the corporate etiquette that applies to writing and sending prompt thank-you or follow-up notes to the person who interviewed them (Catalyst, 1980). The rule has an important functional value. The longer you wait, the more likely you will be to forget to send the note at all.

Make an effort to learn the names of your colleagues, supervisors, subordinates, and clients as quickly as possible. You should also try to recognize the sound of your boss's voice on the telephone. In addition, you should realize that there are no purely social events in the business world. All behavior at office parties is considered job related. Alcohol consumption can lead to imprudent comments and actions.

Overeating and poor table manners will definitely be noted. Failure to observe good manners demonstrates a lack of respect for others and a lack of self-discipline, which could have an impact on your chances for advancement.

Problems you may face in the workplace

Hazing, harassment, and discrimination. New hires are sometimes targets of forms of hazing, which can consist of unnecessary or excessive workloads or subtle but persistent criticism. New hires may be asked to work overtime or to do menial tasks that are not included in their job description. They may be patronized by their supervisors or subtly ridiculed by co-workers. New hires are sometimes viewed as perfect victims during a sort of initiation period. If you ever believe you are the victim of hazing, talk with your immediate supervisor or manager about it. If you feel uncomfortable talking to someone in your company, find a mentor outside your firm. Nothing can be changed until you act to clear the air.

Sexual harassment is an occupational hazard that many employees experience. The definition of sexual harassment includes any repeated or unwanted verbal or physical sexual advances, sexually explicit derogatory statements, or sexually discriminating remarks made by someone in the workplace that are offensive or objectionable to the recipient, cause the recipient discomfort or humiliation, or interfere with the recipient's job performance. The worker who is unfamiliar with ways of dealing with this form of occupational extortion and who does not know where to go for help may experience a considerable amount of stress. Make sure the company policy concerning sexual harassment and methods of redress for grievances is posted. If it is not, you can obtain information on how to handle sexual harassment from the Equal Employment Opportunity Commission office in your area. Remember, sexual harassment and other forms of discrimination are against the law.

Sex or race discrimination is not always easy to identify but is usually very damaging. Occasionally, a recently hired employee cannot be certain whether poor performance evaluations, lack of career development opportunities, and constant criticism are actually the result of unlawful discrimination. The employee may have to wait and observe how others are being treated before making a complaint. Progress has been made in reducing discrimination based on race, sex, or age. However, there are still many issues to be re-solved. The business sector is beginning to realize the extent of the problem, in terms of lowered productivity and increased incidents of conflict and stress. Many businesses and public agencies have issued antidiscrimination policy statements and have established realistic procedures for the redress of grievances.

Poor performance evaluations. In the workplace, supervisors are constantly evaluating job performance. They expect that work will be completed on time without excuses, according to the operating procedures of the organization or priorities of management. If performance does not meet expectations and the employee does not improve, drastic measures may have to be taken. There can be immediate and serious consequences from poor job performance. Being fired, of course, is the most drastic. When a student, you are usually under less stress as a result of poor grades or failed courses because these rarely cause dismissal. The opportunity to improve does not come as easily or as often in the workplace as it does in college.

If you happen to receive a poor evaluation, don't panic. Consult with your supervisor immediately to find out specifically what the problems are and how they can be worked out to your mutual satisfaction. Establish specific goals to meet in a specific time frame. Encourage your supervisor to evaluate your work daily and invite trusted co-workers to help, if possible. In short, try as best you can to fix what is wrong as quickly as possible.

Being fired. As a job applicant, once you have passed through the rigorous selection process that includes interviews with prospective supervisors, a match should be made between your qualifications and the requirements and traits valued by the organization. Sometimes, however, even in the best managed companies, a mismatch does occur for a variety of reasons.

If this happens to you and you are dismissed, it is important to learn the reason behind your dismissal. If you are concerned about improving your performance on the next job (and you should be!), it is necessary to make a realistic evaluation of the situation. For example, the problem may have involved conflict with your supervisor or co-workers that might not exist in another organization. There may have been a discrepancy between the level of skill actually required for a position and your ability, a problem that might not occur again. Or your personal expectations, interests, or values may have interfered with your performance.

Whatever the case, assessing your real strengths and weaknesses will prove an important, though perhaps a difficult, task. Remembering that a trait one person sees as a valuable resource another may find a distinct disadvantage, reevaluate your goals and qualifications to make sure they are consistent with what you want to do. Seek advice from a career counselor, if necessary, to reassess your career direction or improve your on-the-job skills.

The following are steps to take in seeking a new job after being dismissed from one:

- Identify the real problem(s).
- Evaluate your strengths, weaknesses, values, and needs.
- Identify your resources and support.
- Examine alternative solutions.
- Select a viable strategy. Divide it into manageable tasks.
- Enact your plan. Carry out each task.
- Evaluate the outcomes.
- Begin again, if necessary.

Conclusion

Recall from chapter 8 of this book the suggestion that to compete successfully in the job market with business majors you must, as a psychology major, be able to demonstrate that you have acquired 4 basic attributes that are vital for an entry-level position:

- understanding goal-directed behavior
- understanding problem solving
- ability to communicate with others
- understanding human behavior.

Some of these general attributes and skills can be acquired through psychology courses, others in business courses, and still others through job experience.

Courses in personality theory, human motivation, learning theory, industrial/organizational psychology, sensation and perception, and research methodology, among others, should expose you to case studies and problems that reflect actual situations in business. You also need critical courses in other disciplines whether you plan to go to graduate school or decide to try a business career after graduation. By now you are aware of the need for computer skills and practice in oral and written communication. Communication skills will help you make clear, coherent, and persuasive statements and teach you to respond effectively to questions, especially those asked in an adversarial manner. You'll need to learn to write with clarity, precision, and conciseness. The more experience that you get in writing reports and making presentations, the more closely your scholastic preparation will prepare you to meet the needs of employers.

References

Allaire, Y., & Firsirotu, M. (1985, Spring). How to implement radical strategies in large organizations. *Sloan Management Review*, pp. 19-34.

The Catalyst Staff. (1980). *Marketing yourself: The Catalyst guide to successful resumes and interviews.* Toronto: Bantam Books.

PART 6

Issues
of interest
to special
groups

Chapter 17

Women in psychology

Characteristics of women who study psychology

The number of women in psychology graduate programs, like those in other professional fields, has escalated dramatically. Although the number of women who aspire to careers in psychology remains modest compared with many other professions, the proportion of women students obtaining degrees in psychology has increased substantially. Between 1920 and 1972, approximately one-fifth of psychology graduate students were women. In contrast, almost one-half of the students in most psychology graduate programs are now women, and women represent approximately 30% of the students in industrial/organizational psychology and two-thirds of the students in developmental psychology. This trend follows the increase of women among bachelor's degree recipients in psychology. In 1973-1974, the proportion of degree recipients who were female exceeded 50% for the first time and by 1981-1982 nearly two-thirds of bachelor's degrees in psychology were awarded to women (Scientific Manpower Commission, 1984).

In 1981, a study of 9,000 college students was conducted, which included a small number of senior women who planned to pursue doctorates and become psychologists. The results of a substudy that compared women who aspire to careers in psychology with those aspiring to careers in other professions (business, communications, science, law, or medicine), in terms of their family backgrounds, career motivations, self-concepts and self-esteem, and experiences with stress, are described here. The career roles of women who have already completed their degrees in psychology is also considered.

Questionnaires were mailed to 1,200 second-semester senior women from the class of

The section titled "Characteristics of women who study psychology" was adapted from a manuscript written by Diana M. Zuckerman, Subcommittee on Human Resources and Intergovernmental Relations, U.S. House of Representatives, Washington, DC. The section titled "Career issues" was adapted from a manuscript written by Patricia W. Lunneborg, University of Washington.

1981 at seven very selective liberal arts colleges. Two-thirds of the women who received questionnaires responded. Of these respondents, only 24 (3%) of the randomly selected women aspired to careers in psychology. The questionnaires focused on life goals, family background, career motivations, experiences and responses to stress, self-esteem, and self-concepts.

What the substudy found was that future women psychologists are similar to their women counterparts who aspire to other careers in terms of family background and positive feelings about themselves. However, there are some dramatic and interesting differences in self-concepts, career values, and experiences with stress. Women who aspire to careers in psychology are more altruistic and people-oriented. They report somewhat greater concerns with stress in their intimate relationships. They describe themselves as being more cheerful, understanding, and popular with women. They also report lower math and science ability than do premedical students, and lower leadership and public speaking ability than future businesswomen and lawyers. Compared with future businesswomen and lawyers, future psychologists are more likely to report that they respond to stress with symptoms of anxiety.

There is a consistent pattern indicating that future women psychologists tend to emphasize interpersonal relationships in their values, self-concepts, and worries. They are similar to other women majoring in the social sciences who aspire to medical or law careers and consistently different from those aspiring to scientific careers or doctorates in other fields. Despite the competition they will face in gaining acceptance into graduate programs and finding jobs or the stress they will experience in clinical practice, future female psychologists do not see themselves as especially academically gifted, self-sufficient, or able to cope with stress.

Overall, it is unfortunate that, judging from the results of this substudy, so few women aspire to careers in psychology. However, it is encouraging that women who want to be psychologists report more altruistic values and a more positive self-concept in terms of their abilities to interact well with others. It is also important to note that they are not noticeably more emotionally distressed than their classmates.

Career prospects for women psychologists. What kinds of jobs await women psychologists? The most recent statistics show that women are still a minority in psychology, especially in faculty positions and higher paying jobs. In a study of members of the American

Psychological Association (APA) conducted in 1978, 91% of the men and 75% of the women holding doctorates in psychology were employed full-time. In addition, 84% of the men with master's degrees and 63% of the women with master's degrees were employed full-time (Russo, Olmedo, Stapp, & Fulcher, 1981). These employment statistics apparently do not reflect choice; women are more likely than men to be looking for jobs. Minority women are more likely to be employed full-time than are White women. At the master's degree level, women are more likely to teach at universities than men but are less likely to work in business or government. At the doctoral level, women are more likely to work in schools and other educational settings below the university level, whereas, again, men are more likely to work in business or government settings.

Since half of all APA doctoral members obtained their degrees in the 1970s, the difference in postdoctoral work experiences of the men and women is only 2.3 years. As expected, differences in years of postgraduate experience lead to salary differences between male and female psychologists. However, even when postgraduate experience and employment settings are equal, men generally earn more than women. This is true among those with master's degrees as well as those with doctorates. The gap between salaries for men and women is greater than the gap between the salaries for White and Black psychologists. However, among minorities, women psychologists earn more than men.

In academia, women are especially underrepresented in faculties of graduate departments in psychology: Only 23% of these faculty were women in 1983-1984 (Scientific Manpower Commission, 1984). In all programs, women are less likely to be tenured, more likely to have lower academic rank, and more likely to have part-time appointments (Russo et al., 1981). These differences in salary and faculty positions are similar to those found between men and women in other fields. However, the rapid entry of women into the field of psychology during the last decade has not yet been felt at all academic and professional levels. It is likely that differences will narrow as more women enter the positions in which they make the decisions regarding salary and tenure for other psychologists.

Career issues for women psychology majors

So as a woman psychology major, how should you proceed? As you may recall from chapter 5 and other chapters throughout this book, it is essential that you work out a plan for your future by establishing career goals that will help you choose what direction to take in college and beyond. Often job interviewers ask, What do you see yourself doing 5 years from now? 10 years from now? They want to know whether you have a long-range outlook, well-thought-out career goals, and realistic goals in relation to your training and background. To be able to answer these questions, you should adopt a lifespan approach toward your education and career. Your first step in doing this should be to recognize the barriers you face as a woman psychology major and then decide how to overcome them.

Barriers to career development. A personal barrier that has been common among women (and men) psychology majors is math anxiety. As a consequence, the required statistics course in psychology was dreaded, postponed, or not enjoyed. This was also their reaction to general college mathematics classes needed to enter many graduate fields. Another personal barrier is the overwhelming interest women psychology majors have exhibited toward social service positions or people-related occupations and the lack of interest they have shown in technical, data-related occupations. Thus, women graduates were competing with one another for scarce and low-paying social service and education positions, whereas men graduates looked for jobs in occupations across the board. Men with psychology degrees do not hestitate to apply for such technical jobs as computer programming, systems analysis, and human factors engineering.

A social barrier women face is the salary discrepancy that persists between men and women among psychology BAs, MAs, and PhDs in the workforce. The field of psychology is no different than the rest of the professional world as far as the salary gap is concerned, and there is the same disproportionate lack of women at higher management levels. For example, in higher education, women in psychology are concentrated in the lower, untenured instructor and assistant professor ranks, with men in the higher, tenured professorial ranks. And as a result of their overriding interest in helping others, the areas within psychology to which women gravitate are counseling, clinical, developmental, and educational psychology, while women are underrepresented in physiological, experimental, industrial, and measurement psychology.

Juggling parenthood and a career may pose major problems and barriers for many students. They may intend eventually to interrupt their careers or graduate education for marriage and childbearing. There are all kinds of factors (economic, biological, geographical,

professional, etc.) that will affect the time and substance of these decisions. Among women who have attained great personal satisfaction and career success, many continued professional training until their mid-twenties, initiated their careers for 3 to 4 years, had children in their early thirties, then resumed their careers. Others have had very different life patterns and achieved equal success. As a woman plans her career development, she must weigh complex and numerous variables.

Overcoming the barriers. To overcome any math anxiety you might have or lack of technical or business skills, supplement your major. Here is a list of supplementary courses you might consider taking.

> Business administration, management, marketing, law, finance
>
> Technical writing, business communications
>
> Accounting, statistics, mathematics
>
> Computer programming, data processing
>
> Public speaking

As mentioned in chapters 4 and 8, supplementing your major with marketable courses can help you with job hunting later on.

As you tackle some of these courses, boost your self-confidence by using the resources around you: Take an assertiveness training seminar, a math anxiety workshop, a noncredit time management course; work for a political organization in need of fundraisers; or join the student chapter of a professional organization in search of new members. Working steadily on overcoming personal barriers to career development is as important as any class.

Consider exploring employment areas in science, technology, and sales. Science and technology involve no more curriculum shifting than the courses listed previously, and selling is learned on the job. Women psychology majors are already turning from social service to organizational careers because the business world is where the bulk of jobs for all college graduates are. However, there are two powerful obstacles within any organization you should be aware of—the shunting of women to low, dead end, clerical positions and the lack of promotions. Overcoming obstacles requires assertiveness, mentors and sponsors, a supportive network of other women, and visibility.

Develop leadership ability. As a student it just means taking responsibility within a college organization, coordinating and completing projects. The best extracurricular activities for women are those that develop teamwork and leadership skills.

As for the barrier of the earnings gap—get an advanced degree. It means earning more money, prestige, degrees of freedom, promotions, and respect. There are lots of advanced degrees besides those in psychology that are appropriate for psychology majors. In the past, fewer women majors than men have gone on to graduate school. Women have underestimated their abilities and seemed to have lower self-esteem. Men psychology majors are not more intelligent than women majors—but when you believe you can accomplish more, you do.

For women going on to graduate school within psychology, the areas of greatest opportunity are those in which women are underrepresented. However, to be competitive in applying to these graduate programs, women must take courses and do research in these areas, such as in animal experimental, quantitative, industrial, sensation and perception, and physiological psychology.

A plan of action. Back to that interview question. What employers want to be especially sure of is that applicants do not have an "until" orientation; that is, I plan to do such and such "until" I get married, "until" my husband finishes school, or "until" I have children. If you need help in setting goals, this book will help. To determine the steps needed to achieve your goals, go back and read Parts 1 and 2 of this book as well as chapters 13 and 14 on resume and interviewing preparations. A plan of action is not carved in stone. It can always be modified and revised to reflect the changes in you and what you want from life. It shows that you are always in control of your life. A plan is tangible proof that you have the solutions to career issues and problems in your own hands.

References

Russo, N. F., Olmedo, E. L., Stapp, J., & Fulcher, R. (1981). Women and minorities in psychology. *American Psychologist, 36,* 1315-1363.

Scientific Manpower Commission. (1984). Professional Women and Minorities.

Chapter 18

American Indians and Alaska Natives in psychology

The need for American Indian psychologists

Although many young American Indians may come into contact with American Indian teachers, nurses, social workers, or lawyers, few know American Indian psychologists. However, job opportunities on reservations and in urban areas are increasingly available to qualified American Indian applicants trained in psychology. Counselors in alcohol-related programs, diagnosticians in school systems, and therapists for mental health programs are in demand by the Indian Health Service, the Bureau of Indian Affairs, tribal organizations, and public institutions serving American Indian populations. There is a great need for adequately trained administrators for these psychologically oriented programs. The scarcity of American Indian psychologists exists partly because of special difficulties faced by American Indian students. The purpose of this chapter is to identify common obstacles and to suggest ways of overcoming them.

Common obstacles faced by American Indian students

American Indian students face difficulties in college as a result of cultural differences. Values, identity, aspirations and motivations, ability to cope with change, academic preparation, and interpersonal relationships are often cited as areas in which American Indian students differ from other students.

Values. Many American Indian students have difficulty in coping with the challenges of college because they come from cultures that hold educational values different from those of the dominant culture. For example, some American Indian students may learn to view

This chapter was written by Damian A. McShane, Director, American Indian Graduate Training Projects, Utah State University.

excelling in school as standing above peers and thus undesirable. Yet, achievement may be viewed as a means of becoming competent enough to do something useful for the world, community, family, or self. Often young American Indians are confused by conflicting values and arrive at school without a clear, unified sense of their own values. Furthermore, American Indians lack experience with realistic role models, have little personal contact with adults who can help them make career decisions, or have had little experience fulfilling responsible roles. Not having a consistent value system already worked out often means that the student must spend significant emotional energy to develop one, thus distracting him or her from what personal resources should be applied toward school achievement. The ability to organize and direct your energies, which arises from knowledge of your own values, is essential to success in college.

Identity. American Indian students may often wonder whether friends and family like them or whether the skills they have or are acquiring are important to parents and peers. They may end up doubting their self-worth. Such students may not have a detailed knowledge of their community's history and culture or a clear geographical center, such as a place to call home. These uncertainties typically are only symptoms of low self-esteem, which can undermine the confidence and energy the student needs to succeed in college.

Aspirations and motivations. American Indian students may lack professional role models who are psychological service providers in their community whom the students can emulate. Alcoholism, developmental disabilities, divorce, and foster placement of children within the reservation or urban neighborhood are a few of the problems common in American Indian communities. Currently there are few American Indians who are trained as psychological service providers to resolve these problems; therefore, American Indian students have little opportunity to observe what psychologists do and thus have no impetus to aspire to psychology.

Coping with change. Coping with change is critical to the success or failure of American Indian students. Enmeshed in relationships between two disparate cultures, American Indian students are pressured to relinquish their cultural identity; struggle to maintain their cultural integrity while becoming part of the dominant culture; reject the dominant culture by withdrawing or resisting actively or passively; or experience the dominant culture only marginally. These forces can significantly hinder the relationships between personal aspirations and effective use of the educational system. For example, many American Indian students return home to participate in traditional activities or ceremonies during times that are also critical to their studies. Other students become embroiled in political issues to such a degree that their academic performance suffers.

Academic preparation. Many American Indian students simply may not have adequate academic preparation to enable them to succeed in college. Appropriate writing, language, and mathematical skills are particularly important for training in psychology. This lack of preparation may be the case especially for those students who are bilingual.

Interpersonal relationships. American Indian students often come to universities from communal settings with prominent ideological, rather than technical, goals. Although the importance of family and tribal relations on the reservation cannot be overemphasized, the interpersonal aspects of college life often take a back seat to the need to learn technical skills of acquiring facts and information, thinking abstractly outside the context of social life, and communicating with individuals who are not only strangers but whose status and interpersonal relationships with students are undefined. This sort of isolation from interwoven familial and group life can create a sense of alienation.

Overcoming obstacles to success in psychology

Tribal cultural norms differ from those of the larger American society; the success of American Indian students often depends on their ability to reconcile cultural differences. Therefore, as a American Indian student, you must develop a clear value framework. Although there are many points of conflict between tribal cultural norms and the expectations of the larger society, there are also points of harmony between the two. These points need to be emphasized. You need to come to grips with issues of competition versus cooperation, public performance and public discussion of making mistakes, time deadlines, direct and indirect handling of differences of opinion, reacting to constructive criticism, and so on. You should prepare yourself to cope with different kinds of behavior or performance that may be expected of you in college. Your study of psychology may help you see your way through this.

It has been shown that American Indian students who have high self-esteem and a strong sense of identity are more likely to succeed in college. A clear sense of identity often results from an understanding of community history and culture, a sense of home, and a perception of the current and future needs and directions important to the tribal community and to the student's potential place in that future.

A perception of community needs can provide American Indian students with the aspiration to become psychologists. This aspiration can be strengthened by finding and spending time with individuals who are doing what you would like to be trained in to do in psychology. You might help a school psychologist who works with children who have disabilities, a counselor who runs an after-care resource program for alcohol abusers, or a mental health counselor who facilitates a support group. Observing, examining, and discussing specific role and skill requirements (as well as what it takes to acquire the necessary knowledge and skills) with an experienced professional will help you refine your career and schooling expectations.

Once at the university you should secure a mentor relationship with an advanced student or teacher in your area of study. This mentor not only can become the model who can guide you but also the ally upon whom you can rely on to prevent and resolve crises. Often, advisers are assigned randomly to incoming students. However, as you get to know a variety of teachers and university staff, you will find an individual with whom you are most comfortable or who would be good role model. Whether the adviser and mentor are the same person, it is very important for you to secure this relationship and to cultivate it.

As early as possible, join university groups that will provide you with interpersonal and professional relationships. The psychology club, student associations (American Indian and others), sports teams, and social groups are all possibilities. Schedule periodic visits home so that they do not interfere with school but still meet your personal needs to restore family and tribal group relationships. Talk and write to family and friends to help them understand what you are doing and to maintain the interpersonal ties that you have with your community. Volunteer for work in areas related to psychology in your tribal community during school breaks to keep in touch as well as to expand your academic development.

Succeeding as an American Indian psychologist

American Indian students who have been successful in college have been able to adapt to a variety of situations or circumstances into which they are thrust. Whether situational distractions are long-distance travel, ending a friendship, death or illness in the family, or financial hardship, American Indian students who succeed are those who have the strongest commitment to a specific goal that is important to them. They are able to clarify potentially conflicting values, such as learning the old ways versus moving up the ladder of success, maintaining anonymity versus individual visibility in excellence, harmony versus mastery. Some American Indian students have initiated cooperative study groups, which have challenged the belief that being ruggedly and individually competitive is necessary for academic success. Other students have learned to be selective about particular political issues and action before they take priority over academic preparation. It is, as always, important for you to maintain a balance.

There is a great need for trained American Indian psychologists. Many job openings in all parts of the country have gone unfilled because of the lack of qualified American Indian applicants. Your eventual success as a American Indian psychologist begins with your being able to adjust and cope with the demands and forces of the academic life. Once you have succeeded there, the world is wide open for your talents as a psychologist.

Chapter 19

Asian Americans in psychology

Obstacles facing Asian Americans considering psychology

As an Asian American student majoring in psychology, you will need to deal with a variety of issues. Assuming that your family retains an Asian cultural orientation, you may be faced with a feeling that they think you are majoring in a marginal field. In some Asian languages, there is no exact word for psychology. Psychology in many Asian countries today is still struggling for recognition. You may need to be prepared to share your knowledge with your parents, grandparents, and aunts and uncles in terms they can understand. In some instances, the scholarliness of the field can convey that it is intellectually appropriate. In others, the various graduate specialties highlight job opportunities. In other instances, the growing body of knowledge directly relevant to psychology and topics concerning ethnic minorities can provide a contact point. In some cases, the presence of a faculty member who is Asian American conveys a certain reassurance that the field is a valid one. However, if your family expresses concern, you will need to be prepared to express you own reasons for selecting psychology. If you have chosen psychology for the right reasons, prepare yourself to be patient and understanding of your family's concerns. Their interest is stirred by their desire for you to have the best life possible with your talents.

Keep open the possibility, however, that you may really have not selected psychology appropriately. As you read in chapter 3, there are a variety of fields and professions that assist people. Social workers, attorneys, nurses, day-care personnel, teachers, and ministers are all in the business of helping people. You should use all your personal and local resources to

Material for this chapter was contributed by Richard M. Suinn, Colorado State University.

help you decide about your major and what career direction you wish to take. This book is a good starting point and offers beneficial information on how to proceed. Chapter 2 is particularly helpful in assessing your abilities and experiences to help you choose your major. Other chapters look at specific information on career goal setting and on dealing with the resources and staff of your campus career placement center. It might be helpful to look at the educational history of a distinguished Asian American psychologist in order to see what directions he took to arrive at choosing psychology as his major and career.

Profile of an Asian American psychologist

After a successful academic high school education, he enrolled in a local university. However, beyond knowing that he was a natural for more academic studies, he really did not have any strong sense for a major and had not received any vocational counseling. Being bright and competent, he soon learned, did not guarantee making a sophisticated vocational choice. The world of science became his immediate, though not well-considered, choice. He declared a medical technology major on the admission application, changed to physics on the day of freshman orientation, then to chemistry by the start of classes. One semester of chemistry was enough for him to realize that he had best look elsewhere.

What was going on? First, his selection of science, including the early medical science choice, reflected family standards. There was no explicit pressure on him to become a doctor, but he knew that by choosing a medical science degree, his folks would be pleased. Additionally, there was a sense that majoring in another field would mean wasting intelligence on unchallenging ventures. The standard was to achieve the highest levels; society and family defined science as representing such levels.

Selecting psychology as his major, then, came about because he realized that intellectual curiosity can be channeled into curiosity about the human being. The interest in orderliness that was the attraction to the formulas of chemistry fit some of the course content of psychology as well, such as the paradigms of Hullian learning and the psychometric methods and concepts underlying psychological test construction. A major event was discovering that he did not need to choose a field that was worthwhile or valuable or respectable as defined by society's stereotypes. He realized that psychology is indeed a science and has specialties ranging from the applied science to theory construction to mathematical and statistical developments. The topic of psychology is always the human being; the laws that are developed inevitably are relevant to people. At the same time, there is an important role for the student who is less interested in relating to people and more interested in the laboratory or even in computer simulations.

To consider psychology as a major, as this psychologist did, may be difficult for the majority of Asian American students. The bunching up of Asian American students in the engineering and science majors today is due to a number of factors. Many of these students are following their aptitudes for mathematics, or physics, or engineering. A number have been encouraged by earlier successes in science fairs and have therefore given less attention to their equal competencies in less-reinforced skills. Some are responding to the stereotype that Asian American students are truly scholarly and are less outgoing. Possibly there is still the desire to succeed and to accept the current societal definitions of what fields are considered valuable and worthwhile. Parents who have themselves been in business or nonscientific occupations tend to hope that their children will carry the family name to further levels of achievement.

On being an Asian American student

Studies of ethnic minorities have recognized the importance of identity. Because you look different from the majority culture, you have to confront this difference for yourself. If your family retains traditional values, you may already be evaluating where your identity falls. Some Asian Americans elect to have an Asian background and value system as their primary identity. For others, a purely Western orientation has been chosen. In some cases, biculturalism is more descriptive. Such Asian Americans may feel more kinship with other Asians and Asian values but also accept certain Western standards and aspirations. None of these approaches to identity are without gratifications and conflict. You may be faced with making decisions in college in terms of your identity.

As more and more universities accept that ethnic minorities contribute important diversity to their campuses and view such diversity as a positive part of the educational experience for all students, your minority status can become a source of visibility. Although you may not feel Asian or different, or may wish to go unnoticed, you may occasionally find your ethnicity identified, such as in a sociology course on culture. Interested faculty may assume that you are an expert in not only Asian values, but also Asian philosophy and Asian history. If you have become personally comfortable with your ethnicity, then such interest would be relatively easy to handle. If you are knowledgeable about Asian affairs, then you can share your knowledge; if you are not, you can discuss the stereotype that assumed that you are an expert and how you feel about being viewed in this manner. If you have not resolved your identity, then the experience might become a valuable stimulus for you to introspect more on the matter.

Asian American students tend to shy away from viewing themselves as minorities. The term may connote negative perceptions that Asian Americans wish to avoid, such as being poor, underprivileged, militant, or foreign. Asian Americans are physically different in appearance; others do react to these differences; there are stereotypes, some of which are intentionally derogatory; there has been evidence of overt prejudice. But being labeled as an ethnic minority does not simply suggest negative association. Asians do have a separate cultural history with special values that can be identified within the United States. Thus Asian Americans do fit the two definitions of an ethnic minority: a group with physically distinctive features that are different from those of the dominant culture that has maintained certain unique cultural mores or traditions; and a subgroup that has experienced discrimination (for instance, Asian Americans receive less income even though their educational levels are higher).

The obligations and privileges of being Asian

You will be involved in certain situations by being Asian, even if you dress, eat, talk, and behave as a Westerner. If another dormitory resident is experiencing personal difficulties in adjusting and is an Asian American, you might be asked to offer support. You will need to wrestle with your feelings about this. Spend time clarifying your own feelings, then decide how to respond. Ultimately, your major contribution might be in just offering to be a friend. As an example, an Asian American intern was rushed into the psychiatric ward by a frantic psychiatrist, on the premise that the intern could communicate in Chinese to a newly admitted Asian patient. Although the intern was Asian American, he was not bilingual. So the request was as inappropriate as asking a person from Washington State advice on predicting volcanic eruptions, just because Mount Saint Helens once erupted in Washington. For the patient's sake, the intern did locate a

friend who could converse in the right dialect. Later the intern did concede that he regained some respect for the psychiatrist for at least being sensitive enough to try to do something rather than ignoring the patient entirely.

You may inherit the positive stereotype associated with Asians, which includes being hardworking, responsible, quietly efficient, well mannered, and studious. If this stereotype fits you, it will help you go far in clubs, committees, and organizations. If not, and the circumstances warrant, you may need to enable others to recognize you for what you are as an individual. Your major effort may be solely to achieve being understood as a unique person, irrespective of how this relates to general minority issues.

In some settings, including graduate admissions or applications for scholarships, your special status as an ethnic minority may be important. How do you deal with this? What you are facing may be the mixed issue of personal identity, personal values and commitments, or personal philosophy. If you are bicultural or Asian in identity, you would permit yourself to be recognized in this way. If you feel you are primarily Western but believe that you can serve as a model to others by doing well with scholarship or succeeding in training, you may feel comfortable in the circumstance. On the other hand, if your personal philosophy is to refuse any special treatment, or you believe that your personal characteristics should not influence decisions, you might not have any interest in such opportunities. The limited resources such as scholarships or specialized training programs such as those in cross-cultural psychology should require the student applicant to prove his or her unique ethnic identity via activities. Yet, in many settings, Asian Americans do not receive their rightful share of services, financial support, or training simply because of a failure to apply or a distorted sense of pride at not being needy or a minority.

Ethnicity in psychology

Until recently, the study of ethnicity did not receive the acceptance it rightfully deserved. However, several events have occurred. First, professional journals and conferences have now accepted research, symposia, and workshops on ethnicity as a variable influencing human performance and achievement. Second, volumes are now appearing on cross-cultural or culturally sensitive counseling and psychotherapy. Third, courses devoted to minority content and research are now offered in many universities, treating the subject as legitimate scientific findings rather then as a social advocacy issue. Fourth, the American

Psychological Association (APA) membership formally recognized the importance of ethnicity by forming the Board of Ethnic Minority Affairs, which takes leadership in matters such as identifying ethnic minority resources, developing ideas for education and training, initiating further scientific research endeavors, and promoting culturally sensitive delivery systems. The membership has elected two minority persons to be presidents of APA. Fifth, in addition to participating in the efforts of APA, Asian American psychologists have also organized their own professional association, the Asian American Psychological Association. And finally, the National Institute of Mental Health sponsored the National Asian American Psychology Training Conference, in recognition of the importance and needs of Asian American psychologists.

Studying ethnicity within psychology

In the event that you wish to become involved in ethnicity studies, there are many avenues for you to pursue regardless of what specialty you elect within the field of psychology. For example, if you eventually specialize in the branch of experimental psychology dealing with cognitions or information processing, you might eventually study the influence of bilingualism on concept formation or decision making among Asian Americans. If you select work in developmental psychology, you might examine the role of family approaches to discipline as they relate to performance of Asian American children. If you become interested in clinical psychology, you could devote attention to the ways in which different cultures provide coping resources or the effects of folk treatment approaches for abnormal behaviors.

How can you best prepare for your future studies in ethnic psychology? As a start, discover your roots. Find out how your parents' generation perceives and thinks about life, what values are involved in their decisions, and how their decisions are made. Engage in those aspects of tradition that offer you more perspective, such as an Asian church. Observe your familial environment with fresh eyes: Are there activities that represent culture and meanings you had overlooked? Seek out and compare reactions of Asian Americans and non-Asians to the same events, to learn about similarities and differences. Further, be alert for those who can provide oral histories, an intriguing source of information that may not be found in books.

On campus, take advantage of Asian American student services or Asian American student organizations. Remember that the student services are not only for students in academic or financial trouble, but can be a locus for people sharing similar ethnic characteristics. It can also be a resource for achieving more information, such as arranging for visits from Asian touring performance groups, or for special speakers, or for involvement with research projects. Do not overlook the non-Asian faculty and students who are doing things that may stimulate your own growth and identity. The professor who teaches Asian literature, philosophy, or geology may provide insights, even though he or she might not be Asian. People of other ethnic backgrounds might engage you in discussions about their own thoughts or beliefs that can raise topics equally important to you.

Find out who has written on subjects of interest to you by talking to faculty. Start to identify common themes, conflicts, or issues that psychologists are studying related to Asian Americans. See if you can identify recurring names of experts, especially those who are themselves Asian Americans. Engage in projects that lead you to become involved. Help plan activities or locate resources for an Asian Awareness Week, including defining the goals you think should be met by this endeavor. Select a term paper topic associated with ethnicity for your courses in and outside of psychology. Volunteer to do special studies research projects with a faculty member who is sympathetic and interested in ethnicity. Enroll in courses that offer a scientific foundation from different viewpoints, such as sociology, anthropology, literature, philosophy, and political science. If you are not bilingual, you may consider some exposure to conversational language classes.

If you live in a community with a large Asian population, do volunteer work in nursing homes, crisis centers, or Asian American counseling centers. Attend case conferences, training presentations, or public speeches in Asian psychology sponsored by the community agency. Befriend an Asian American graduate student. Find out about his or her plans and interests in psychology. Seek advice about undergraduate experiences and what opportunities to take advantage of before graduation. Establish links with major organizations. Ask to be on the mailing list of groups, such as APA's Board of Ethnic Minority Affairs. Become a student member of the Asian American Psychological Association and attend meetings. And finally, by all means retain a balance. Ethnic psychology does not exist in a vacuum. Learn all you can about the basic foundation material of psychology. Then expand your horizons to include material on ethnicity and continue to let your horizons expand!

Chapter 20

Blacks in psychology

Why should Black students major in psychology?

Generally, psychologists are concerned with the thought and behavior of people. They try to describe processes of thinking, language development, socialization of values, and attitudes. Psychologists want to understand why some people experience mental and emotional anguish that results in behaviors that are personally destructive at worst and dysfunctional and unproductive at best. However, the application of the discipline to Black people has not always been adequate. Thus, in the past, few Black students have considered psychology as a major.

Recently, however, the number of Black students earning psychology degrees has increased significantly. Many have focused their attention on issues affecting Black people on the premise that racism is a fact of American life that is responsible for many of the major problems Blacks face. Furthermore, it has been recognized that understanding problems specific to Black people leads to greater understanding of other aspects of society as well. So why should you major in psychology? The simple answer is that the science and profession of psychology need you. If any of the following statements arouse your curiosity and make you ask why, psychology may be the major for you.

- Over 60% of all Black babies born in the United States are born to mothers who are teenagers.

- Over 40% of all prison inmates are Black.

- Among corporate managers in major U.S. corporations, Blacks are 28% more likely to leave their jobs during a given year.

- Melanin, a substance responsible for pigment coloration and prominent among

Material for this chapter was contributed by James M. Jones, American Psychological Association, Washington, DC.

Blacks, is also a precursor to serotonin, a drug used to treat schizophrenia.

- It has been argued that race is no longer as significant as economics in determining opportunities for Black Americans. It has also been argued that there is no distinctive Black culture apart from the culture of poverty.

- Black students on predominantly Black college campuses perform better than their Black counterparts on predominantly White campuses.

- Black adolescents who adopt a militant style in confronting racism in the United States experience greater stress than those who choose to either ignore or remain passive about racial issues.

Applying psychology to helping Black people

As you have read throughout this book, the field of psychology offers a wide range of career possibilities. The question you face is, at what level do you want to apply your knowledge of psychology? As you may recall, a psychologist is one who has earned a doctorate. Thus, one of the first decisions you need to make is whether you want to attain a doctoral degree. If you do, this book contains lots of information on how you should proceed. Chapter 15 gives advice on maintaining a good grade-point average, gaining research experience, preparing for the GREs and MATs, selecting graduate programs, and applying for financial aid. However, if you are not interested in attaining an advanced degree in psychology, there are many important and interesting careers you can enter with a BA in psychology. You might want to read over chapters 8, 9, and 11 for some career possibilities and chapters 13 and 14 for guidance tips.

In short, Black psychologists do what any psychologist does. And as a psychologist, you have many options. You can address the problems of Black people directly as a researcher, therapist or counselor, school psychologist, teacher or professor, consultant, or program administrator. Most Black psychologists do combinations of these activities. Careers in industry, government, and private practice provide the largest incomes. You are limited only by your energy, imagination, and time.

A brief scenario of a Black psychologist's own career development can give you an idea of the wide range of experiences and opportunities available through psychology. This distinguished Black psychologist began his career by running rats in the research laboratory of his undergraduate professor. Hired as an engineering psychologist (with a BA degree only), working for the Franklin Institute of Philadelphia, he conducted multidimensional scaling studies of radar controllers and designed simulated decision-making games based on the Vietnam War. After receiving a master's degree, he studied how the value of coins influenced the psychophysical judgments of their size (dimes were overestimated and pennies were underestimated). He then entered a doctoral program to study the problems of racism and the development of Black people in America; however, he chose to study attitude change and the psychology of humor. After taking an academic job, while continuing to study the physiological correlates of laughter and humor, racial differences in performance of Black and White athletes, and the minority content of public television programs, he spent a year in Trinidad, West Indies, studying calypso and carnival.

Following the publication of his book on prejudice and racism and another on a Black NFL football player, he joined a private consulting firm and conducted program research for the federal government. The American Psychological Association (APA) then hired him as an administrator and program manager of the Minority Fellowship Grant to conduct an extensive investigation of the turnover of minority managers in major U.S. corporations. Later, he returned to teaching as a professor in psychology.

By this example, you can see the wide range of activities possible within the field of psychology. Therefore, you should consider (a) how you want to spend your adult working life; (b) what career you can find in which you can both help others and feel fulfilled and creative; and (c) what life-styles and associated economic requirements you envision. Psychology permits you to fulfill all three considerations if you are creative, hard-working, motivated, and plan intelligently and effectively.

Special advice to Black students

Psychology is a science and a profession, organized to promote each in the service of human welfare. For you to pursue psychology as your major and career, take the advice offered throughout this book as a first step. The advice can be applied effectively by all students majoring in psychology. However, as a Black student majoring in psychology, there are some special resources for you to call on that can help on your road to success. These resources are not exhaustive but can be of great help to you in addressing the problems of Black people.

The Association of Black Psychologists, founded in 1969, continues to provide a focus that directly involves its members in issues of relevance and critical importance to the Black community. The Association has organized testimony and expert witness presentations on issues of testing, jury selection, and Black child development and abuse. It has regional divisions and holds an annual convention during August. You will certainly want to maintain your contact with the Black community and your Black psychology colleagues through this association.

There is also representation of Black and other ethnic group concerns within APA. The Board of Ethnic Minority Affairs (BEMA) represents the policy issues that affect ethnic minority citizens as well as psychologists. Your interest and concern with Black psychological issues will also gain support through APA's National Policy Studies, which organizes testimony on issues that affect the psychological community and the concerns of organized psychology. The profession of psychology is an important one that welcomes you not only as a practicing psychologist (teacher, researcher, or whatever you choose) but as a member of national associations that help to focus your expertise and concerns.

So now you know that there are important problems of Black life that need to be addressed by you. Your undergraduate psychology degree is the first step. Do well, set up mentoring relationships with faculty and others, prepare for graduate study, gain admission to a program of your choice, and apply for adequate financial support. Select a training program that confers tangible skills, and point yourself toward a career with flexibility, foresight, and energy.

Chapter 21

Hispanics in psychology

The field of psychology, both as a science and profession, is young and growing. The field has an influence on many aspects of human life, from health care to industry. Psychologists now work not only in traditional areas such as clinical psychology but also in diverse areas such as engineering, aerospace, business, and law. And as the field of psychology continues to expand, it has a greater influence on the study of ethnic groups. For Hispanics, psychology can offer help with their growing needs. For Hispanic students, psychology can offer an ever-expanding range of career opportunities for those who find they have an interest and aptitude for entering the field.

Although Hispanics in the United States represent one of the nation's many cultural minority groups, recent statistics from the Bureau of the Census reveal a picture of an emerging population with growing needs.

- Hispanics are united by a common Spanish language and cultural heritage but are diverse in terms of geography, country of origin, race, class, and circumstances surrounding their entry into the country.

- There are more than 14 million Hispanics (Mexican American, Puerto Rican, Cuban American, or Central American) now living in this country. Hispanics have tripled in numbers over the past 3 decades.

- The median age of Hispanics in the United States is substantially lower than that of the general population, 23 years as compared with 30 years. Over half of all Hispanics in this country are under the age of 34.

- Because of the lower average age of Hispanic females, the birth rate is also very high.

- Since the 1960s, Hispanics have become the dominant immigrant group in the United States, now representing 42% of all immigrants entering the country. This percentage

Material for this chapter was contributed by Richard C. Cervantes, University of California at Los Angeles.

does not include estimates of undocumented immigrants.

- It is expected that by the year 2000, Hispanics will be the largest of all minority group populations in this country, comprising about one-fourth of the total population.

These figures tell the story of a population that is young, diverse, and growing at a rapid pace. Many researchers sense that the social, political, and economic impact of this growth in the nation's Hispanic population is already apparent. Just as with any other growing population, increased social and economic demands require a greater understanding of the characteristics of this population. The Hispanic student choosing a career in psychology has an opportunity to become involved in the progress of Hispanics either at the individual level, such as providing mental health services, or at the community level, such as conducting research to improve public policy.

The need for Hispanics in psychology

There is a tremendous need for young Hispanics to enter the field of psychology. Recent surveys suggest that less than 2% of all psychologists are Hispanic. One of the primary problems in both the practice of psychology as well as in Hispanic psychological research is the lack of people who are well acquainted with Hispanic culture. This is especially true in the area of mental health. Numerous studies show that many Hispanics prefer not to go to community mental health agencies because of the lack of trained bilingual-bicultural therapists. This underutilization is extremely detrimental for society. Many mental illnesses simply go untreated. In California, where the Hispanic population is nearly 5 million, the number of qualified Hispanic psychologists lags far behind the needs of the community.

School psychology is another area of psychology that is grossly underrepresented. Problems arise when language and other cultural characteristics are mistaken for learning deficits of young school-age Hispanic children. Many Hispanic children are placed in special learning classes that often hamper their achievement and success later on. Qualified Hispanic bilingual-bicultural school psychologists are needed to help otherwise normal Hispanic children rid themselves of the stigma of inferiority simply because of language and cultural differences. There is need for research in this area as well. Many researchers argue that the present educational system does not foster success among Hispanic children. This

may be most evident in the high number of Hispanic youth who never finish high school. Certainly this issue needs further research so that the exact nature of the problem can be understood. Sensitivity to these culturally relevant educational issues is best addressed by Hispanics who themselves are sensitive to the problems.

Many other research opportunities for Hispanic psychologists are available. In addition to conducting mainstream psychological research, the Hispanic psychologist has the opportunity to conduct research of a cross-cultural nature. We are just now beginning to uncover the influence of Hispanic culture in areas such as psychotherapy, bilingualism, education, stress-related disorder, cognition, and a host of other areas that traditionally have not been addressed in past psychological research. What is also needed is research that helps identify differences found within Hispanic culture, not just viewed from a Hispanic cultural perspective. One promising area of psychological research, for example, is that of investigating what effect immigration has on mental health. What are the effects of prejudice and discrimination that are often experienced by new immigrants? Are there mental health problems that are specific to Central American refugees as opposed to other Hispanic immigrants? From a psychological research perspective, there are many questions that would be best addressed by researchers who are familiar with Hispanic culture. The need for both Hispanic researchers and service providers has grown and will continue to grow with the tremendous growth in the nation's Hispanic population. Opportunities for Hispanic psychology majors are many, and these opportunities will continue to expand.

Success strategies for Hispanic psychology undergraduates

As an undergraduate student in psychology, you should begin developing a strategy for success. The best way to go about doing this is to follow the advice in this book. Although your Hispanic background provides you with a unique perspective and different challenges, the guidelines here are effective for everyone. Your strategy building is, however, contingent on whether you are going on to graduate school. If you are not, certain strategies can help improve your marketability following graduation. Reread Part 2 of this book for insights on psychology and career preparation. Most crucial to improving your marketability is becoming a well-rounded student. It may be advantageous to complement your psychology degree with a minor in another related area of study. For advice on this approach, read chapter 4.

Should you choose to go on to graduate school, the best advice is to be well prepared. Follow the guidelines set forth in chapter 15. Although many graduate programs express a desire to recruit minority students, do not assume this to be the case. Rely on your own merits. Talk with your psychology professors, especially those who conduct cross-cultural research. You may be fortunate to work with a Hispanic professor who cannot only share research interests but also can serve as a guide by sharing his or her experiences as a Hispanic student in psychology.

Although there are many paths to successful completion of undergraduate and graduate education, few Hispanics have chosen to become professional psychologists. This is a challenge for you, one that requires diligence and hard work, but one that is rewarding in terms of personal achievement and the contribution you can make to improving the lives of many Hispanics through your research or service activities.

Chapter 22

Reentry of men and women in psychology

Between 1972 and 1982 the increase in enrollment of college students aged 18 to 24 was 23%. However, the increase among students 25 to 34 was 70% and, among students 35 and over, 77% (Grant & Snyder, 1983). In psychology these increases among older students are probably greater, given that the field meshes well with certain personal motivational factors, such as self-improvement and career changing, that are of greater importance to returning students than to 21-year-old baccalaureates entering the job market for the first time (Reehling, 1980). This chapter addresses some of the problems and concerns you may face as a reentering student and offers advice. The chapter is aimed at people in their 40s, including women whose children are old enough to get along without as much attention and men able to retire after 20 years of a first career.

Career problems to overcome before the bachelor's degree

The quantitative deficit. Returning students of both sexes typically have a verbal advantage over younger students (a better vocabulary and greater reading comprehension), but are usually at a disadvantage in quantitative skills. Many returning students avoid college majors and courses that rely on mathematics. Thus, reentry students in overwhelming numbers choose majors in the humanities and social sciences.

The psychology curriculum is very attractive to older students except for one course, statistics. Many returning students put off taking statistics until the very last, thus denying themselves statistical knowledge that would make all their other psychology courses easier. If you lack sufficient quantitative skills, you should start all over again in mathematics.

Material for this chapter was contributed by Patricia W. Lunneborg, University of Washington.

Your academic adviser can recommend remedial courses, help locate tutors, and suggest study partners and math anxiety workshops. Students who take remedial work in mathematics open up new possibilities for themselves in terms of college courses, jobs, and graduate programs. The statistics course ceases to be an obstacle, and a master's degree becomes a real possibility.

A self-defeating sense of urgency. Many reentry students feel a need to acquire their bachelor's degree immediately. As a result, many sign up for more courses than they can handle or ignore prerequisites and get in over their heads. As an older student, you need to be reminded that it takes just as long as it does for younger students to study adequately, acquire research experience, and put in hours of fieldwork.

Readjusting your life. Reentry students typically adjust too slowly to going back to school. It takes time to acknowledge all the adjustments that must take place. The first year back to school can be confusing for families until proper arrangements are finally set in place. If a reentry student tries to hold on to an old job and go to school, the result can be disastrous.

Building your self-esteem. Going back to school can be a real blow to an older student's self-esteem. Can I still learn? What if I fail? Why are the instructors so young? How can I compete with those kids? What if they make fun of me? However, a new identity as a psychology major is necessary for eventual success as a job hunter—a job hunter with a new employment objective, new skills and knowledge, and new goals for life.

Ask your department's academic advisers to put you in touch with other older students. Organize a conversation hour devoted to reentry. Form a support network of older psychology students, drawing up a list of addresses and phone numbers. There is no better way to build self-esteem than to share your successes with people who understand and reveal your failures to people who will laugh with you, not at you.

Career problems to overcome after the bachelor's degree

An entry-level job. Older students are no different from younger students when they start out in a new field. They are asked to start at the bottom and work their way up. Many reentry students with experience cannot tolerate

this idea. But overcoming personal resistance to starting over again can be worth it. Usually, the experience and skills you acquire before going back to school can be added to your psychology degree to lend to swift promotions. However, you might desire to settle for a longer (one year or more) job search that includes successful job-hunting tactics, many of which are written about in this book. See chapters 13 and 14 for information on how to proceed. Also, look into many of the excellent resources on this subject listed in chapter 23. An example of an actual successful job-hunting tactic was that of an older graduate, a secretary of 15 years, who was told by employment agencies that secretarial work was all she was qualified for. She wrote a letter of recommendation for a person qualified for management, based on business experience and college training, closing by saying the person was herself. This letter landed her a job that led rapidly to manager of personnel (Berman, 1980).

Too old for graduate school. You are never too old for graduate school. Graduate programs are not biased against older students. Some even prefer them. The problem to overcome, again, is that sense of urgency that says you can't afford to spend time in college. If an older student desires to acquire a master's or PhD in psychology, and in all the important ways (grades, GRE scores, research, experience) is qualified, he or she should go for that degree. Read chapter 15 for more details on pursuing a graduate degree.

Immobility. All psychology majors, no matter what their age, need to apply to graduate programs across the country to guarantee that they will be accepted somewhere and to ensure that they will be accepted in a program that matches their interests and values. You can wait a lifetime trying to get into a local program when to have studied 1,000 miles away would have meant being back home in four years with a PhD. Even more tragic is to get into a local program that is mismatched with your goals and personality. Reentry students of both sexes are often adamant about the fact that they cannot seek further education or employment anywhere else because of family. If opportunities are better in other parts of the country, it is certainly worth a serious family discussion of the possibilities for growth and advancement for everyone by overcoming misperceived immobility.

What psychology departments should do for you

Psychology departments should take the lead in recognizing that not all students are 18 to 22, live near campus, have no nonacademic responsibilities, have adequate study skills, and lots of time to study (Hooper & March, 1980). Departmental advisers should provide you, the reentry student, with individualized, special counseling that ensures that you receive sufficient information about campus resources. Ask your adviser to help you get social support from peers, employment on campus if you must work, remedial courses, tutoring and study skills help, and a niche in the department by working closely with a faculty member, by lending teaching or research assistance. Advisers need to be aware that reentry students may not necessarily be more mature, even though they may look more mature than younger students. Remember to seek advice when you need to; to use student health services (you've paid for them) and tutoring resources; to take remedial mathematics; and to seek a graduate degree if you desire and are qualified.

References

Berman, E. (1980). *Re-entering: Successful back-to-work strategies for women seeking a fresh start.* New York: Crown Publishers.

Grant, W. V., & Snyder, T. B. (1983). *Digest of education statistics, 1983-84.* Washington, DC: National Center for Education Statistics.

Hooper, J. O., & March G. B. (1980). The female single parent in the university. *Journal of College Student Personnel, 21,* 141-146.

Reehling, J. E. (1980). They are returning: But, are they staying? *Journal of College Student Personnel, 21,* 491-497.

Chapter 23

Resources

This chapter contains valuable resource information for the bachelor's candidate in psychology. Books and journal articles are grouped by topics, which correspond to the topics of each chapter. A list of organizations and societies, with descriptions and addresses, follows.

Is psychology for you?

American Psychological Association. (1983). *Psychology as a health care profession.* Washington, DC: Author.

American Psychological Association, Division of Consulting Psychology. (1980). *Consulting psychology.* Washington, DC: Author. (Available from APA Division of Consulting Psychology, 631 A Street, SE, Washington, DC 20003)

American Psychological Association, Division of Military Psychology. (Undated). *Military psychology: An overview.* Washington, DC: Author.

Cates, J. (1973). Baccalaureates in psychology: 1969 and 1970. *American Psychologist, 28,* 262-264.

Davis, J. (1979). Where did they all go? A job survey of BA graduates. In P. Woods (Ed.), *The psychology major: Training and employment strategies.* Washington, DC: American Psychological Association.

Henderson, C., & Ottinger, C. (1984). *Employment prospects for college graduates.* ACE Policy Brief. Washington, DC: American Council on Education.

Kulik, J. A. (1973). *Undergraduate education in psychology.* Washington, DC: American Psychological Association.

Malin, J. T., & Timmreck, C. (1979). Student goals and the undergraduate curriculum. *Teaching of Psychology, 6,* 136-139.

Stapp, J., & Fulcher, R. (1982). The employment of 1979 and 1980 doctorate recipients in psychology. *American Psychologist, 37*, 1159-1185.

Stapp, J., & Fulcher, R. (1983). The employment of APA members: 1982. *American Psychologist, 38*, 1298-1320.

Titley, R. W. (1978). Whatever happened to the class of '67? *American Psychologist, 33*, 1094-1098.

Psychology and career preparation

Babaric, P. (1980). "What do they really want?": A survey of undergraduates' preferences and aversions in psychology. *Canadian Psychologist, 21*, 84-86.

Boltuck, M., Peterson, T., & Murphy, R. (1980). Preparing undergraduate psychology majors for employment in the human service delivery system. *Teaching of Psychology, 7*, 75-78.

Edwards, J., & Holmgren, R. (1979). Some prerequisites for becoming a "really" applied social psychologist. *Personality and Social Psychology Bulletin, 5*, 516-523.

Fretz, B. R. (1976). Finding careers with a bachelor's degree in psychology. *Psi Chi Newsletter, 2*, 5-9.

Gold, M. (1980). Training for off-campus psychology: A cautionary tale and some elements of a model. *Academic Psychology Bulletin, 2*, 309-319.

Lunneborg, P. W., & Wilson, V. M. (1982). Job satisfaction correlates for college graduates in psychology. *Teaching of Psychology, 9*, 199-201.

Norcross, J. C., & Wogan, M. (1982). Undergraduates as researchers in mental health settings. *Teaching of Psychology, 9*, 89-91.

Prerost, F. J. (1984). Post-graduation educational and occupational choices of psychology undergraduate practicum participants: Issues for the psychology profession. *Teaching of Psychology, 8*, 221-223.

Ross, S. M., Hughes, T. M., & Hill, R. E. (1981). Field experience as meaningful contexts for learning about learning. *Journal of Educational Research, 75*, 103-107.

Sherman, A. R. (1982). Psychology fieldwork: A catalyst for advancing knowledge and academic skills. *Teaching of Psychology, 9*, 82-85.

Ware, M. E., & Meyer, A. E. (1981). Career versatility of the psychology major: A survey of graduates. *Teaching of Psychology, 8*, 12-15.

Weinstein, B. (1985). *What employers look for.* The Honda Guide to Getting a Job. New York: McGraw-Hill.

Psychology majors in the workplace

American Psychological Association. (1978). *Careers in psychology.* Washington, DC: Author.

American Psychological Association, Division of Industrial and Organizational Psychology. (Undated). *Careers in consumer psychology.* Washington, DC: Author.

American Psychological Association, Division of School Psychology. (Undated). *The school psychologist.* Washington, DC: Author.

Carducci, B. J., & Wheat, J. E. (1984). Business: Open door for psych majors. *APA Monitor, 15*, 20.

Careers, Inc. (1982). *Psychologist, school.* Largo, FL: Author. (Address: see below. Cost: $1.00)

Careers, Inc. (1983). *Psychologist, clinical.* Largo, FL: Author. (Address: see below. Cost: $1.00)

Careers, Inc. (1983). *Counselor, school.* Largo, FL: Author. (Address: see below. Cost: $1.00)

Careers, Inc. (1984). *Psychologist.* Largo, FL: Author. (Address: P.O. Box 135, Largo, FL 34294-0135. Cost: $1.25)

Catalyst National Headquarters. (1975). *Psychology* (Career Opportunities Series No. C-19). New York: Author. (Address: 14 East 60th Street, New York, NY 10022)

Catalyst National Headquarters. (1975). *Psychology* (Education Opportunities Series No. E-19). New York: Author. (Address: see above)

Chronicle Guidance Publications. (1982). *Psychologists* (Occupational Brief No. 144). Moravia, NY: Author. (Address: P.O. Box 1190, Moravia, NY 13118-1190)

Lunneborg, P. W. (1974). Can college graduates in psychology find employment in their field? *Vocational Guidance Quarterly, 23*, 159-166.

Lunneborg, P. W. (1985). Job satisfactions in different occupational areas among psychology baccalaureates. *Teaching of Psychology, 12*, 21-22.

Lunneborg, P. W. (1985). *Putting the liberal arts to work.* Seattle: University of Washington.

Roe, A. (1956). *The psychology of occupation.* New York: John Wiley.

Rudman, J. (1980). *Psychologist* (Career Examination Series No. C-627). Syosset, NY: National

Learning Corp. (Address: 212 Michael Drive, Syosset, NY 11791)

Super, D. E., & Super, C. M. (1982). *Opportunities in psychology* (4th ed.). Skokie, IL: National Textbook. (Address: 4255 West Touhy Avenue, Lincoln, IL 60646)

Task Force on the Employment of Experimental Psychologists in Industry. (1985). *Scientific and technical careers in psychology.* Washington, DC: American Psychological Association.

Presenting yourself to employers

Bolles, R. N. (1982). *The advanced quick job-hunting map.* Berkeley, CA: Ten Speed Press.

Bolles, R. N. (revised annually). *What color is your parachute?* Berkeley, CA: Ten Speed Press. Definitive guide for effective job seeking. Excellent reference for first-time job seekers and career changers. Fun to read, too.

Bostwick, B. E. (1985). *Resume writing: A comprehensive how-to-do-it guide* (3rd ed.). New York: Wiley. Up-to-date guide on resume writing for all job seekers. Provides examples of ten basic resume writing styles and how each can be used in a variety of occupations. Summarizes important aspects such as what is a resume, who uses resumes, why it's important to write one, what should be included and excluded, appropriate language, and resume faults.

Career Options Projects. (1982). *For your action: A practical job search guide for the liberal arts student.* Bloomington: Indiana University, Arts and Sciences Placement Office. Along with basic job search techniques this reference includes good sample resumes, lists of action verbs, and an organizational worksheet for resume preparation. Good general reference for psychology majors because of its liberal arts orientation.

Catalyst Staff. (1980). *Marketing yourself.* New York: Bantam Books. Presents a thorough treatment of resume preparation, including how to determine job targets, analyze achievements, and critique resumes. Focuses on women job seekers.

College Placement Council. (revised annually). *College placement annual.* Bethlehem, PA: Author.

Crystal, J. C., & Bolles, R. N. (1980). *Where do I go from here with my life?* Berkeley, CA: Ten Speed Press.

Dickhut, H. W. (1981). *The professional resume and job search guide.* Englewood Cliffs, NJ: Prentice-Hall. Provides special guidelines for students, including good tips for organizing and highlighting areas of knowledge and achievement. Ideas for many different fields.

Irish, R. K. (1978). *Go hire yourself an employer.* York: Doubleday. Solid job search advice includes good tips and exercises for all job seekers on "getting it together" and writing an effective resume.

Jackson, T., & Mayleas, D. (1981). *The hidden job market for the 80s.* New York: Times Books.

Lathrop, R. (1977). *Who's hiring who.* Berkeley, CA: Ten Speed Press. Special chapter offers a unique approach to resume writing, the qualifications brief. Good advice on new ways of catching the employer's eye. Traces the steps of preparing a brief. Excellent, easy-to-read.

Lathrop, R. (1980). *Don't use a resume.* Berkeley, CA: Ten Speed Press. This is the workbook from *Who's hiring who,* an elaboration of the qualifications brief chapter. An outstanding reference.

Lunneborg, P. W., & Wilson, V. M. (1982). *To work: A guide for women college graduates.* Englewood Cliffs, NJ: Prentice-Hall.

McLaughlin, J. E., & Merman, S. K. (1980). *Writing a job-winning resume.* Englewood Cliffs, NJ: Prentice-Hall. Shows step-by-step approach for generating a positive self-image and communicating that image to employers. Offers creative ideas for presenting special skills, education, and experience. Provides dozens of case studies and sample resumes.

Nadler, B. J. (1985). *Liberal arts power! How to sell it on your resume.* Englewood Cliffs, NJ: Prentice-Hall. The emphasis on liberal arts makes this one of the most useful reference books for psychology graduates. Easy to read, very thorough, explains the whys and hows of its point of view, provides many options and good advice on aesthetics.

U.S. Department of Labor. (1977). *Dictionary of occupational titles* (4th ed.). Washington, DC: U.S. Government Printing Office.

U.S. Department of Labor. (1979). *Guide to occupational exploration.* Washington, DC: U.S. Government Printing Office.

U.S. Department of Labor. (1981). *Selected characteristics of occupations as defined in the Dictionary of occupational titles.* Washington, DC: U.S. Government Printing Office.

U.S. Department of Labor. (1982). *Supplement to the Dictionary of occupational titles.* Washington, DC: U.S. Government Printing Office.

U.S. Department of Labor. (revised annually). *Occupational outlook handbook.* Washington, DC: U.S. Government Printing Office.

Washington, T. (1985). *Resume power: Selling yourself on paper.* Bellevue, WA: Mount Vernon Press. Easy to understand, step-by-step guide to writing effective resumes. Packed with information and answers to virtually every question that could be asked about resumes. Upbeat presentation, full of examples and solid resume building and use strategies.

Woods, P. J. (Ed.). (1979). *The psychology major: Training and employment strategies.* Washington, DC: American Psychological Association.

Beyond the bachelor's degree

For new hires

Byrne, J. A. (1985). *Let's hear it for liberal arts.* Forbes, 136(1), 112-114.

Cutler, M. M. (1984). *The first (fateful) day.* Unpublished report, Pace University, Lubin Graduate School of Business, New York.

The Editors of Fortune. (1982). *Working smarter.* New York: Viking Press.

Foley, J. M. (1979). Gaining experience by volunteering: Altruism with a plus. In P. W. Woods, (Ed.). *The psychology major: Training and employment strategies.* Washington, DC: American Psychological Association.

Harragan, B. L. (1977). *Games mother never taught you.* New York: Warner Books.

Henning, M., & Jardim, A. (1977). *The managerial woman.* Garden City, NY: Anchor Press/ Doubleday.

Neugarten, D. A., & Shafritz, J. M. (1980). *Sexuality in organizations: Romantic and coercive behaviors at work.* Oak Park, IL: Moore Publishing Company, Inc.

Pascale, R. (1984). Fitting new employees into the company culture. *Fortune, 109*(11), 20-24.

Peters, T. J., & Waterman, R. H., Jr. (1982). *In search of excellence.* New York: Harper & Row.

Port, O. (1985). Where the jobs will be. *Business Week's guide to careers, 3*(3), 60-63.

Trahey, J. (1977). *Jane Trahey on women and power.* New York: Rawson Associates Publishers, Inc.

Weinman, G. (1984). *Corporate communication skills: An assessment of current training needs.* Unpublished report, Fairleigh Dickinson University, English Department, Madison, NJ.

Woods, P. J. (Ed.). (1976). *Career opportunities for psychologists: Expanding and emerging areas.* Washington, DC: American Psychological Association.

Zambrano, A. L., & Entine, A. D. (1976). *A guide to career alternatives for academics.* New Rochelle, NY: Change Magazine Press.

Graduate psychology

American Association of State Psychology Boards. (Undated). *Entry requirements for professional practice of psychology: A guide for students and faculty.* New York: Author. (Available from the Office of Professional Affairs, APA, 1200 17th Street, NW, Washington, DC 20036)

American Psychological Association. (Rev. biannually). *Graduate study in psychology and associated fields.* Washington, DC: Author.

The College Board, College Scholarship Service. (1984). *The college cost book: 1984-85.* New York: Author.

Feingold, S. N., & Feingold, M. (1982). *Scholarships, fellowships, and loans* (Vol. 7). Arlington, MA: Bellman Publishing Co. (Address: P.O. Box 164, Arlington, MA 02174)

Fretz, B. R., & Stang, D. J. (1980). *Preparing for graduate study: Not for seniors only!* Washington, DC: American Psychological Association.

Graduate and professional school opportunities for minority students 1975-1977 (6th ed.). (1975). Princeton, NJ: Educational Testing Service.

Kesslar, O. (1983). *Financial aids for higher education* (11th ed.). Dubuque, IA: William C. Brown. (Address: 2460 Kerper Blvd, Dubuque, IA 52001)

Knox, W. J. (1970). Obtaining a PhD in psychology. *American Psychologist, 25*, 1026-1032.

Livesey. H. B., & Doughty, H. (1975). *Guide to American graduate schools* (3rd ed.). New York: Viking.

Macmillan Editors. (1983). *The college blue book* (Vols. 1-3). New York: Author.

Mealiea, W. L. (1973). The unquestionable value of a master's degree for a PhD-pursuing student. *American Psychologist, 28*, 938-939.

National Academy of Sciences, National Research Council. (1980). *A selected list of fellowship opportunities and aids to advanced education for United States citizens and foreign nationals.* Washington, DC: National Science Foundation. (Available from Publications Office, National Science Foundation, 1800 G Street, NW, Washington, DC 20550)

Rosser, M. (1970). Criteria used for admission by graduate departments. *American Psychologist, 25*, 558-560.

Saccuzzo, D. P., & Schulte, R. H. (1978). The value of a terminal master's degree for PhD-pursuing students. *American Psychologist, 33*, 862-864.

Schoonmaker, A. N. (1971). *A student's survival manual.* New York: Harper & Row.

Scott, W. C., & Davis-Silka, L. (1974). Applying to graduate school in psychology: A perspective and guide. *JSAS Catalog of Selected Documents in Psychology, 4,* 33. (Ms. No. 597)

Test study guides

A description of the Advanced Psychology Test. (1979). Princeton, NJ: Educational Testing Service.

Bulletin of information and list of testing centers with 60 practice items for the MAT. (revised annually). New York: Psychological Corporation.

Graduate Record Examination Aptitude Test (4th ed.). (1975). New York: Arco.

GRE information bulletin. (1979-1980). Princeton, NJ: Educational Testing Service.

How to pass the MAT. (1967). New York: Cowles Education Corporation.

Millman, S., & Nisbett, R. E. (1966). *Psychology: Advanced test for the GRE.* New York: Arco.

Issues of interest to special groups

Brandenberg, J. B. (1974). The needs of women returning to school. *Personnel and Guidance Journal, 53,* 11-18.

Carnegie Commission on Higher Education. (1971). *Less time, more options.* New York: McGraw-Hill.

Conversations with returning students. (1967). Ann Arbor: University of Michigan, Center for Continuing Education for Women.

Hiestand, D. (1971). *Changing careers after thirty-five.* New York: Columbia University Press.

Johnson, D. H., Weiss, K. L., & Sedlacek, W. E. (1977). *A comparison of the needs of returning and traditional students by sex* (Counseling Center Research Report 13-77). College Park: University of Maryland.

Manis, L. G., & Mochizuki, J. (1972). Search for fulfillment: A program for adult women. *Personnel and Guidance Journal, 50,* 594-599.

Tidball, M. E., & Kistiakowsky, V. (1976). Baccalaureate origins of American scientists and scholars. *Science, 193,* 646-652.

Troutt, R. (1972). *Special degree programs for adults: Exploring nontraditional degree programs in higher education.* Iowa City, IA: American College Testing Program Publications.

Valley, J. R. (1973). *Increasing the options.* Princeton, NJ: Educational Testing Service.

Women's Bureau. (1974). *Continuing education for women: Current developments.* Washington, DC: U.S. Department of Labor, Employment Standards Administration.

Organizations

The American Psychological Association

The American Psychological Association (APA) is a society of scientists, teachers, and professionals organized by charter to advance psychology as a science and as a means of promoting the public welfare. Its membership in 1985 was approximately 62,000. The Association publishes scientific and professional journals and holds an annual convention to promote communication and exchange of new knowledge among psychologists. Many APA boards and committees devote their attention to a wide variety of concerns, ranging from the social and ethical responsibilities of psychologists to their education and training.

The national efforts of APA are greatly facilitated by regional, state, and local associations of psychologists. State psychological associations are particularly active in representing psychologists' professional and scientific interests to state legislators and other policymakers. The addresses and the offices of these associations may be obtained by writing to the Governance Services Office, APA, 1200 17th Street, NW, Washington, DC 20036.

Divisions of the APA

The numerous interests of psychologists are represented within the APA by 45 divisions. Psychologists who belong to the APA usually join one or more divisions. Most divisions publish a journal, a newsletter, or both. Information about divisions and their publications may be obtained from the division secretaries, whose addresses are listed each November in *American Psychologist,* a journal published by APA. Addresses of division secretaries and newsletter editors are also available from the Governance Services Office, APA, 1200 17th Street, NW, Washington, DC 20036.

1. General Psychology
2. Teaching of Psychology
3. Experimental Psychology
5. Evaluation and Measurement
6. Physiological and Comparative Psychology
7. Developmental Psychology
8. Personality and Social Psychology

9. Society for the Psychological Study of Social Issues
10. Psychology and the Arts
12. Clinical Psychology
13. Consulting Psychology
14. Society for Industrial and Organizational Psychology
15. Educational Psychology
16. School Psychology
17. Counseling Psychology
18. Psychologists in Public Service
19. Military Psychology
20. Adult Development and Aging
21. Applied Experimental and Engineering Psychologists
22. Rehabilitation Psychology
23. Consumer Psychology
24. Theoretical and Philosophical Psychology
25. Experimental Analysis of Behavior
26. History of Psychology
27. Community Psychology
28. Psychopharmacology
29. Psychotherapy
30. Psychological Hypnosis
31. State Psychological Association Affairs
32. Humanistic Psychology
33. Mental Retardation
34. Population and Environmental Psychology
35. Psychology of Women
36. Psychologists Interested in Religious Issues
37. Child, Youth, and Family Services
38. Health Psychology
39. Psychoanalysis
40. Clinical Neuropsychology
41. Psychology and Law
42. Psychologists in Independent Practice
43. Family Psychology
44. Society for the Psychological Study of Lesbian and Gay Issues
45. A Society for the Psychological Study of Ethnic Minority Issues—A Division of APA
46. Media Psychology
47. Exercise and Sport Psychology

Other APA Sources of Information

APA Membership Directory: Biographical, geographical, and divisional membership listing of APA Fellows, Members, and Associates. Published every 4 years.

APA Membership Register: Lists names, addresses, and states as Fellow, Member, or Associate in APA and its divisions. Published in years when the Directory is not.

APA Monitor: A monthly newspaper containing news about the field of psychology, APA, and behavioral science legislation.

Psychology Today: A monthly magazine for the general public containing articles and news about psychology and behavioral sciences.

PASAR: APA also operates the Psychological Abstracts Search and Retrieval (PASAR) system. PASAR provides a computer-generated bibliography consisting of citations and abstracts from the PsycINFO database and the PsycALERT File, tailored to the individual researcher's requirements.

Honor societies

Psi Chi

Psi Chi, the National Honor Society in Psychology, recognizes excellence in scholarship by graduate and undergraduate students in psychology. It provides the opportunity for early involvement and recognition in psychology. Membership is through chapters located at accredited colleges and universities that have met Psi Chi's standards. To join, undergraduates must rank in the upper 35 percent of their class and have completed a specified number of credits in psychology. Graduate students must have at least a "B" average. A registration fee pays for lifetime membership. The *Psi Chi Newsletter* is published quarterly. For further information, contact Psi Chi, 1400 N. Uhle Street, Rm. 703, Arlington, VA 22201.

Psi Beta

Psi Beta is the honor society in psychology for students who attend 2-year colleges. Psi Beta teaches students, before they transfer to a 4-year institution, that honor societies and related activities are important to their development as psychology students. Write or call the Educational Affairs Office, APA, 1200 17th Street, NW, Washington, DC 20036, for the name of the current president.

Special group organizations

Women

• APA Committee on Women in Psychology
• Association for Women in Psychology

For the name of the person to whom to write at these two organizations, write or call the Women's Program, APA, 1200 17th Street, NW, Washington, DC 20036.

Minorities

Minority Fellowship Program

Funded jointly by the National Institute of Mental Health and the APA, the minority Fellowship Program awards fellowships to individuals of ethnic minority background for graduate study in psychology leading to the doctorate. The program also advises students, faculty, and administrators on behavioral science and mental health issues related to ethnic minority populations. For more information, write or call the Minority Fellowship Program, APA, 1200 17th Street, NW, Washington, DC 20036.

Other Resources

- APA Board of Ethnic Minority Affairs
- Association of Asian-American Psychologists
- Association of Black Psychologists
- National Coalition of Hispanic Mental Health and Human Services Organizations
- National Hispanic Psychological Association

For information about these organizations, write or call the Ethnic Minority Affairs Office, APA, 1200 17th Street, NW, Washington, DC 20036.

Organizations for fields related to psychology

There are many careers in fields related to psychology. The following organizations can provide you with information about the careers suggested by their names.

American Anthropological Association
1703 New Hampshire Avenue, NW
Washington, DC 20009
(202) 232-8800

American Association for the Advancement of Science
1515 Massachusetts Avenue, NW
Washington, DC 20005
(202) 467-4400

American Council on Education
One Dupont Circle
Washington, DC 20036
(202) 833-4700

American Medical Association
535 North Dearborn Street
Chicago, IL 60610
(312) 751-6000

American Orthopsychiatric Association
19 W. 44th Street, Suite 1616
New York, NY 10036
(212) 354-5770

American Association for Counseling and Development
5999 Stevenson Avenue
Alexandria, VA 22304
(703) 823-9800

American Psychiatric Association
1400 K Street, NW
Washington, DC 20005
(202) 682-6000

American Sociological Association
1722 N Street, NW
Washington, DC 20036
(202) 833-3410

National Academy of Sciences National Research Council
2101 Constitution Avenue, NW
Washington, DC 20418
(202) 334-2000

National Mental Health Association
1021 Prince Street
Alexandria, VA 22314
(703) 684-7722

National Association of Social Workers
7981 Eastern Avenue
Silver Spring, MD 20910
(301) 565-0333

National Education Association
1202 16th Street, NW
Washington, DC 20036
(202) 833-4000

Publication Inquiries National Institute of Mental Health
5600 Fishers Lane
Rockville, MD 20857
(301) 443-4515

Scientific Manpower Commission
1776 Massachusetts Avenue, NW
Washington, DC 20036
(202) 223-6995

Your Responses

Dear Reader:

We invite your comments or suggestions concerning this title. Did you find the information helpful? What else would you like to have discussed? Please write your comments below and send them to:

American Psychological Association
1400 North Uhle Street, Room 700
Arlington, VA 22201
Attn.: Special Publications

Name: _____

Address: _____

_____

_____

Phone: _____

Looking into Graduate School in Psychology?

Make an Important Decision Easier!

Graduate Study in Psychology and Associated Fields, 1986, with 1987 Addendum

Have all the information you need to make that big decision — which graduate program in psychology to apply to. *Graduate Study in Psychology and Associated Fields, 1986 with 1987 Addendum* provides you with practical information on:

- **Financial Aid**
- **Tuition Costs**
- **Degree Requirements**
- **Application Pointers**
- **Housing Opportunities**
- **Special Facilities and more!**

There are over 600 programs listed with 60 pages of updates and new entries in the addendum. Each program entry contains an extensive description based on questionnaires completed by schools in the U.S. and Canada. *Graduate Study* includes indexes by institution and by the subject specialty of the degree offered. Learn general pointers on applying to graduate school, retraining policies, and licensing — all with this easy-to-use reference.

Make an important decision for your future easier with the help of *Graduate Study in Psychology and Associated Fields, 1986 with 1987 Addendum.* A must for students; libraries; counselors; and department offices in psychology, education, and health administration; and industrial organizations. Order your copy today!

─ ORDER FORM ─ ▬ ▬ ▬ ▬ ▬ ▬ ▬ ▬

Graduate Study in Psychology and Associated Fields, 1986 with 1987 Addendum
Item #4270011

____ Copies at $18.50 List. $ _____
____ Copies at $14.50 APA
     Members/Affiliates. $ _____
        Shipping and Handling $ __2.00__
              Total $ _____
____ Enclosed is my check payable to APA.
____ Charge my __ MasterCard or __ VISA

Card No. _____ Exp. date _____

_____
signature

Name _____

Address _____

_____

City _____ State_____ Zip_____

To order by phone using MasterCard or Visa call (703) 247-7705. No collect calls please.

Send to: **American Psychological Association**
Order Department
P.O. Box 2710
Hyattsville, MD 20784

All orders totalling $25.00 or less must be prepaid. Allow 4-6 weeks for delivery.
Prices are subject to change without notice.